PLATO
STATESMAN

Translation, Introduction,
Glossary, and Essay

THE FOCUS PHILOSOPHICAL LIBRARY

The Focus Philosophical Library is distinguished by its commitment to faithful, clear, and consistent presentations of texts and the rich world part and parcel of those texts.

Thanks to our series advisors:
Peter Kalkavage, St. John's College
Maureen Eckert, University of Massachusetts-Dartmouth
Dustin Gish, College of the Holy Cross

Aristotle: De Anima • M. Shiffman
Aristotle: Nicomachean Ethics • J. Sachs
Aristotle: Poetics • J. Sachs
Athenian Funeral Orations • J. Herrman
Descartes: Discourse on Method • R. Kennington
Empire and the Ends of Politics (Plato/Pericles) • S. D. Collins and D. Stauffer
Four Island Utopias (Plato, Euhemeros, Iambolous, Bacon) • D. Clay and A. Purvis
Hegel: The Philosophy of Right • A. White
Liberty, Equality & Modern Constitutionalism, Volume I • G. Anastaplo
Liberty, Equality & Modern Constitutionalism, Volume II • G. Anastaplo
Lucretius: On the Nature of Things • W. Englert
Plato and Xenophon: Apologies • M. Kremer
Plato: Euthydemus • M. Nichols
Plato: Gorgias • J. Arieti and R. Barrus
Plato: Gorgias and Aristotle: Rhetoric • J. Sachs
Plato: Meno • G. Anastaplo and L. Berns
Plato: Parmenides • A. K. Whitaker
Plato: Phaedo • E. Brann, P. Kalkavage, and E. Salem
Plato: Phaedrus • S. Scully
Plato: Republic • J. Sachs
Plato: Sophist • E. Brann, P. Kalkavage, and E. Salem
Plato: Symposium • A. Sharon
Plato: Theatetus • J. Sachs
Plato: Timaeus • P. Kalkavage
Socrates and Alcibiades: Four Texts • D. Johnson
Socrates and the Sophists • J. Sachs
Spinoza: Theologico-Political Treatise • M. Yaffe

PLATO
STATESMAN

Translation, Introduction, Glossary, and Essay

Eva Brann
Peter Kalkavage
Eric Salem

focus an imprint of
Hackett Publishing Company, Inc.
Indianapolis/Cambridge

Plato *Statesman*: Translation, Introduction, Glossary, and Essay
© 2012 Eva Brann, Peter Kalkavage, Eric Salem

Previously published by Focus Publishing/R. Pullins Company

Focus an imprint of
Hackett Publishing Company, Inc.
P.O. Box 44937
Indianapolis, IN 46244-0937
www.hackettpublishing.com

ISBN: 978-1-58510-290-7

Library of Congress Cataloging-in-Publication Data

Plato.
  [Statesman. English]
  Plato's Statesman : translation, with glossary, essay, and appendices /
Eva Brann, Peter Kalkavage, Eric Salem.
      p. cm.
  Includes bibliographical references (p. 165) and index.
  ISBN 978-1-58510-290-7
  1. Political science--Early works to 1800. 2. Philosophy, Ancient. I.
Brann, Eva T. H. II. Kalkavage, Peter. III. Salem, Eric. IV. Title. V.
Title: Statesman.
  JC71.P3132 2012
  320.01—dc23   2012007529

Contents

For Laurence Berns
friend and colleague
1928-2011

ACKNOWLEDGMENT

We wish to thank Jennifer Behrens for the graphic design of the figures that appear in the appendices and the interpretive Essay. We also wish to thank Professor Dustin Gish for his thorough, insightful suggestions. Our edition owes much to him, both in the general arrangement of sections and in crucial details.

Introduction

"The latent causes of faction are thus sown in the nature of man."

Madison, *Federalist* 10

The *Statesman* is one of Plato's political masterpieces. Like the *Republic* and *Laws*, it addresses questions fundamental to any serious inquiry into politics: Is there such a thing as political knowledge or "science"? If so, what is it, and who is its possessor? Does it confer the ability to rule, allowing its possessor to translate theory into practice whether by advising, or legislating, or actively governing? Of possible regimes, which is best? What is justice, and how is it related to other virtues, in particular, to wisdom? What is human nature, and what sort of education most befits it?

The *Republic, Statesman,* and *Laws* are not, however, confined to political matters. This is most evident in the *Republic,* where Socrates and his friends found a city in speech in order to see justice and injustice in the individual soul (Book 2 and end of 9), and where the conversation eventually rises to the heights of being and the transcendent good (Books 6 and 7). The *Laws* rises above politics at one point to consider the whole of all things, the cosmos, and its dependence on god as the unmoved source of motion and the object of rational piety (Book 10).

The *Statesman,* too, is a blend of political and non-political themes. Its official goal is to define the true *politikos* or statesman—to distinguish him in speech from all other human types with whom he might be confused. But in following the course of this project we encounter many other topics that seem only distantly, if at all, related to political matters, topics fascinating and problematic in their own right. These include the work of definition as the division of things according to kind; knowledge and its various forms; form itself, *eidos,* as that which allows us to recognize a thing as the thing that it is; the practical and productive arts, so important to human life and

1

wondrous in their complex interconnections and devotion to detail; mathematics as the prime instance of knowledge that is clear, orderly, and precise; measurement in relation to the arts and to wisdom itself; myth as an imaginative mode that complements the task of rigorous account-giving; the nature of learning and the dependence of learning on the illustrative power of models or paradigms; human nature and its tendency toward extremes; nature, *physis*, as the realm in which living things are nourished, grow, and reproduce; the difference between the human and the divine; the cosmos in relation to the whole of time.

Great themes, political and non-political alike, occupy the world of Plato's *Statesman*. But the dialogue does not make it easy, especially for the first-time reader, to gain access to them or to understand what exactly is being said about them. Even more than its partner dialogue, the *Sophist*, the *Statesman* immerses the reader in a sea of details having to do with the various arts or *technai*. There are confusing detours in the conversation, abrupt revisions in what is said, and sometimes an apparent lack of direction. It is a strange and confounding work that often seems to be more labyrinth than guiding thread.

Another difficulty in Plato's *Statesman*, one that characterizes all the dialogues but especially the more technically formal ones, is the problem of *tone*: What is to be taken seriously, and what playfully? In reading the *Sophist* and *Statesman*, we sometimes get the impression that Plato intends these expository dialogues, with their amusing neologisms like "psycho-trading" and "the footed-pasturing art," as a parody of technical speech. Plato's fondness for play appears throughout the dialogues: in image and myth, and in Socrates' generally playful way of engaging those with whom he converses. Sometimes play becomes a central theme. In the *Parmenides*, the old philosopher calls his exercise in hypotheses "a workmanlike game" (137B); in the *Timaeus*, physical account-giving is said to be a form of play that provides intelligent relief from the serious business of dialectic (59D); and in the *Statesman*, the stranger refers to play just before he tells his great story about the cosmos (268D). He even goes out of his way to mention playthings, toys, as one of the possessions essential to the city (288C). Play, moreover, is crucial in the accounts of education we find in the *Republic, Statesman*, and *Laws*.

Play, for Plato, is essential to the serious work of philosophy and the search for truth. It is an expression of the flexibility, intelligent openness, and overall musicality of the philosophic temper. But it is hard to know how to take this playfulness in the *Statesman*, where the tone of Plato's central character, the stranger from Elea, is arguably more opaque, more stiffly sober, and harder to read than in the *Sophist*.

The extreme difficulties of Plato's *Statesman* have their benefits. They compel us to reflect on the limits inherent in the philosopher's effort to be precise in speech. They also remind us that political phenomena, which are familiar to everybody and might seem easier to talk about than Being, are in fact overwhelmingly problematic once we examine them closely, and more deeply connected with the question of Being than is first apparent. Finally, the obstacles remind us that "beautiful things are difficult," as the Greek saying goes, and that a commitment to philosophy requires not only an effort to be synoptic—to see things whole and gathered (*Republic* 7, 537C)—but also a willingness to submit to the close inspection of the humblest, seemingly most insignificant details.

The Dramatic Setting: Theaetetus and Sophist

Plato presents philosophic inquiry not in treatise form but through the playful form of dialogue. This form—with its characters and plot, its rootedness in place, time, and circumstance—draws attention to the everyday world that is the context and origin of philosophy. The dialogue form is not just a mask behind which Plato hides his real thoughts. It is the means by which he seeks to involve us as active participants in the conversation, and to arouse our desire for wisdom, our *eros*. The form invites us to connect the speeches we hear with the souls of the various speakers, to examine the strength and the weakness of a character's opinions and arguments, and to gain self-knowledge by critically examining our own opinions and arguments.

The *Statesman* is the third and final entry in Plato's trilogy: *Theaetetus, Sophist, Statesman*. Many important things come up in the two preceding dialogues. The following brief summary may therefore be helpful to our readers, especially if they have read only one, or neither, of the preceding dramas.

In the *Theaetetus*, Socrates converses with the elderly geometer Theodorus and Theodorus' most promising student—the brilliant young Theaetetus, who, according to Theodorus, is Socrates' unbeautiful look-alike (143E-144A). This is the same Theaetetus who was famous for developing the theory of irrational lines in geometry, and for devising constructions of the five regular, so-called platonic, solids. In Plato's dialogue, Theaetetus foreshadows his future glory when, in the company of young Socrates, he defines the *dynamis* or what we call a square root (147D). Socrates urges the young geometer, whom Theodorus praises for his intelligence and his brave and gentle character, to take on the question: What is knowledge? The question is not typical for Socrates, whose questions tend to be about ethical matters and human happiness. The question concerning knowledge sets the stage for the dramas to come. It paves the way for the knowing, professorial stranger, who is confident of his ability to reach definitions through his method of division.

In questioning Theaetetus, Socrates casts himself in the role of a midwife and Theaetetus in the role of one who is pregnant in soul. Socrates will assist in the birth of the young man's opinions, his attempts to answer the question about knowledge. But more importantly he will test those opinions to see whether or not they are sound—whether, that is, Theaetetus' intellectual offspring are worthy of "life" or "death," of being retained and nurtured or rather abandoned. Theaetetus makes several valiant attempts to say what knowledge is: it is perception; it is right opinion; it is right opinion with an account or *logos*. When all these attempts fail, when all of his newborn definitions prove to be, in Socrates' phrase, mere wind-eggs, Socrates proposes that they meet again the next morning. He wants to continue the conversation but now must answer the indictment brought against him by Meletus for impiety and corruption of the Athenian youth. This reference to Socrates' upcoming trial, condemnation, and death brings the *Theaetetus, Sophist*, and *Statesman* into close connection with the *Apology*, in which Socrates gives a public account of his pursuit of philosophy and his curious bond with the city of Athens.

Before leaving the *Theaetetus* we should note that although Socrates' initial question was about knowledge, much of the discussion in the dialogue is devoted to the possibility and nature of false opinion or error. This is why Socrates brings in the sophist Protagoras right at the beginning of his examination of Theaetetus' initial claim that knowledge is perception (151E). He does so, it seems, in order to guard the possibility of false opinion and ignorance by refuting Protagoras' teaching that "man is the measure of all things," which Socrates takes to mean: "each man is the measure of all things." If each man is the measure of all things, then there is no such thing as false opinion or ignorance, in which case Socrates' role as a midwife who judges the worth of opinions, and as the gadfly of Athens, is pointless and absurd. The emphasis on false opinion establishes a direct link between the *Theaetetus* and the *Apology*. It also foreshadows the centrality of error in the *Sophist* and *Statesman*. Both dialogues begin with a reference to an error on the part of Theodorus, and in both the stranger regularly points to errors in the divisions.

When the company meets the next morning as planned, Theodorus has a surprise for Socrates. He brings with him an unnamed *xenos*—a stranger or guest—from Elea, home of the great Parmenides. The stranger, Theodorus explains, is an associate of Zeno and Parmenides and "a very philosophical man" (*Sophist* 216A). Socrates seizes on the opportunity to accuse Theodorus of a possible failure of recognition, a failure to know who the stranger really is. Perhaps he is no man at all, Socrates playfully suggests, but a god in disguise, a "god of refutation" come to Athens to punish philosophers like Socrates for their feeble attempts at account-giving (216B). When Theodorus responds by saying that the philosopher, though not a god, is godlike, Socrates persists in focusing on the difficulty of recognizing genuine philosophers, who, thanks to the ignorance of others, appear in various guises: sometimes as statesmen, sometimes as sophists or professors of wisdom, and sometimes as though they were altogether mad (216C-D).

Socrates then tells Theorodus that he would like to know what people who live in the stranger's region of Elea think about these three: sophist, statesman, philosopher. Do they regard them as one being, or two, or rather as three distinct kinds (*genê*), as the three names indicate? It's easy, the stranger responds, to say that they regard them as three, but not at all easy to define or mark them off "one by one" (217B). The stranger's response suggests a projected trilogy of dialogues: *Sophist, Statesman, Philosopher*. But the sequence ends with the *Statesman*, and the projected trilogy is left incomplete. The reader is made to wonder: Does Plato mean to suggest that the stranger simply abandons his ultimate goal of defining the philosopher? Or is the point rather that a third separate dialogue is now unnecessary, and that the philosopher has somehow been revealed in the pair of dialogues, *Sophist* and *Statesman*?

In the *Sophist*, the stranger and Theaetetus set out to define the wily professor of wisdom. They do so by means of *diairesis*: the method of dividing things according to kind. Theaetetus had used this very method in his effort to define the *dynamis* or square root (*Theaetetus* 147E). Several assumptions are at work here. One is that to know a being is to know the kind or "class" to which that being belongs. This kind stamps the thing to be defined with a characteristic "look" that makes the thing capable of being recognized as the being that it is, and as distinct from all other beings. Another assumption is that kinds are arranged in an intelligible order that can be laid out in speech—a hierarchy of sorts in which some kinds are more comprehensive than others and contain these as sub-kinds. We are reminded of classification in biology, which defines living things in terms of "genus" and "species."

The sub-kinds or species we see in the *Sophist* and *Statesman* may be imagined in various ways: as cuts or divisions within a larger class, or perhaps as specifically distinct "offspring" originating in a common "parent." A diagram of this sort of order would resemble a series of branches emanating from a single point, or a map indicating alternate paths and junctures. Unlike the divisions in the *Sophist*, those of the *Statesman* are more complex and scattered, and cannot be represented by a single picture. The reader will find diagrams of these divisions in an appendix to the present translation. We encourage our readers to consult these diagrams as they work their way through the dialogue. Our hope is that the diagrams will provide a sort of "You Are Here" map of the *Statesman* that will help our readers follow the steps of the division and get a sense of the often-perplexing order of topics.

In the *Sophist*, the stranger illustrates the method of division through an example—the angler. The example offers a presumably lucid instance of what it means to divide kinds in order to reach a definition in the case of a humble and familiar art. It also puts forth the two most fundamental and comprehensive kinds that distinguish the various arts—making and getting, or production and acquisition. This primordial division is the basis for all the divisions to come. Later in the dialogue the stranger adds a third most comprehensive kind of art—separating. This kind brings the sophist to light, wondrously, as a Socrates-like purger of arrogance and false opinion (230A-231A). The angler offers a playfully apt image or likeness of the sophist, who travels from city to city, angling in the marketplace for money and for promising youths who wish to appear wise. The stranger and Theaeteus are also in a sense anglers: they are fishing in the waters of speech for the slippery sophist, who knows how to use this medium to his advantage.

We should emphasize here that the stranger's work of attending to kinds involves collection as well as division—synthesis as well as analysis. The final definition, as we see in the case of the angler, is a summing up or "recollection" of the entire series of cuts, the entire path that leads to the culminating identification of the thing to be defined. The stranger does this regularly in the *Sophist* and *States-*

man: he gathers and counts up all the divisions that had appeared successively in the account.

What is perplexing in this respect is that the stranger defines the sophist seven times. The last definition is the most impressive, the one that compels the stranger and Theaetetus to face and overcome the greatest difficulty: the problem of non-being. But we must not forget the six definitions that precede the last and that locate the sophist in different classes and along different lines. These definitions make us wonder whether the stranger's final definition, impressive as it is, really succeeds in capturing the sophist "in his very being" (268D). Multiple definitions are problematic on the assumption that *diairesis* is supposed to reveal a single look or nature that excludes other looks or natures. But, on the positive side, the definitions, in their manyness, present a true-to-life picture of the sophist as a multi-natured, polymorphous being. His being consists precisely in the many aspects and guises that the stranger's account has faithfully generated. To use a term from ancient Greek astronomy, the stranger has "saved the appearances."

The high point of the *Sophist*—indeed, the metaphysical high point of all the dialogues—is the long section in which the stranger and Theaetetus take on the problem of non-being. The sophist has been identified at this point as a maker of deceptive images or phantasms. He is not really wise but he seems so; he doesn't really have true knowledge but he seems to. He is the human exemplar of an *image*—that is, something that is the likeness of something else and, therefore, is what it is not. In order to render possible the uncanny art of the sophist—that of making deceptive images of truth, illusions in speech—the stranger must defend the possibility of falsehood as the being of what is not, something explicitly forbidden by Parmenides, the stranger's philosophic father (237A). In the central "deed" of the dialogue, the stranger dares to commit parricide, to refute his philosophic father's great teaching about non-being so that the sophist may at last be brought to light (241D).

To save the being of non-being, and thus make falsehood possible, the stranger and Theaetetus embark on an excursion into the realm of the "greatest kinds": Being, Same, Other, Motion, and Rest. They do so because the problem of non-being, which seems at first insurmountable, leads to the no less problematic nature of being. If non-being means "nothing whatsoever," then it can neither be said nor thought, in which case the sophist remains safe and sound within the dark of non-being (254A). The brilliant move on the part of the stranger is to interpret non-being as opposition or *otherness* (258B). Each kind or form is the same as itself and other than all the other kinds or forms. Non-being as otherness pervades the realm of kinds and becomes a formal constituent of the intelligible whole. Indeed, it is the power by which all the kinds distinguish themselves from each other, relate to each other without compromising their self-sameness. Non-being as otherness makes speech, articulation, possible. In particular, it makes it possible to claim that the sophist says what is not, where saying what is not does not mean saying nothing, but rather saying what is other than the truth.

Having apparently solved the problem of non-being, the stranger and Theaetetus return to the work of division. Earlier, the stranger had defined speech through an image that will play a crucial role in the *Statesman*: speech is "the interweaving of the forms" (259E). Here, at the end of the *Sophist*, he returns to this image: he and Theaetetus "tie up" the sophist's name "by interweaving it together from end to beginning." They define the sophist as "an imitator of the wise man" and one who makes phantasms of truth rather than accurate likenesses.

From Sophistry to Politics

In the *Statesman*, the stranger, now accompanied by young Socrates, Theaetetus' friend and gym-partner, pursues the *politikos* or statesman. Our philosophic gaze shifts from a sham knower who hides in non-being to a genuine knower whose nature is high and kingly. For that is what the true statesman is, above all, for the stranger—a knower. The task of *diairesis* will be to define the statesman by exposing the genuine "political science" that is his alone.

As noted above, the *Statesman* is more difficult than the *Sophist*. Its language is more awkward and harder to piece together; the wholeness of the account is more elusive and the stranger's divisions more scattered and complex; the stranger departs from his usual method of dividing only by two; and the myth he tells about the cosmos is bizarre and, by his own admission, out of proportion with its intended purpose. We wonder why an account of the statesman should be more demanding, as it seems, than an account of the sophist, and whether the shift reflects a change in the stranger, or in his respondent, or in the subject matter, or in all three.

As we read the *Statesman*, we must recall the opening of the *Sophist*, where we first meet the stranger from Elea. This opening raises many questions about both dramas in which the stranger appears: Who *is* this stranger, and why has he come to Athens? Why is he never named? Why does Plato set this project of defining the sophist and statesman so close to the time of Socrates' trial? In addition to his goal of answering Socrates' initial question about names and beings, the stranger is clearly engaged in an attempt to educate his two young respondents, both recommended by Socrates: Theaetetus in the *Sophist* and young Socrates in the *Statesman*. We must attend carefully to how this process of education unfolds, to what *happens* at every stage of the drama. Like Socrates in the *Theaetetus*, the stranger seems to be engaged in his own version of psychic midwifery, his own attempt to purge his young respondents of their false opinions. But it is not clear how the formal method of *diairesis* is related to this effort. Nor is it clear what the stranger's relation is to the elder Socrates, who sets the whole drama in motion.

What is the *Statesman* about? This may seem like an absurd question. Doesn't the title speak for itself? And yet, as we have seen, this perplexing and rich work is by no means limited to defining the statesman. Ultimately, the statesman, as we discover, is an occasion for cultivating the habit and discipline of dividing by kind—of becoming, as the stranger says, "more dialectical about all things" (285D). To get the full force of this claim, we should recall the definition of dialectic that the stranger puts forth in the *Sophist*. The possessor of "dialectical knowledge" has proper perception of the One and the Many in the realm of forms. He "thoroughly perceives" (*diaisthanetai*), discerns, how a single intelligible look or idea extends through (*dia*) many, and how a plurality of looks or ideas is embraced by a single look (253D). To draw on the weaving-image that appears in the *Sophist* and *Statesman*, we may say that the dialectical man knows the "fabric" of being. And yet, it is far from easy to see how the method of division is related to dialectic taken in this sense—how *diairesis*, as practiced by the stranger, makes us more capable of "thoroughly perceiving" the weave of One and Many.

We have already touched on several important things the *Statesman* may be said to be about. What follows is a brief summary of a few especially noteworthy elements in the dialogue. We revisit them in the interpretive essay that appears after the translation and glossary. There the various themes and perplexities of the *Statesman* will appear in the context of the dialogue's dramatic unfolding.

The main element in the drama of the *Statesman* is, of course, *division*. This was described briefly in our earlier summary of the *Sophist*. Division according to kind, we must note, is a basic feature of all serious thought. To think properly about anything, we must make careful and accurate distinctions. Failure to do so is either incompetence or sophistry. In the *Sophist* and *Statesman* we witness the formalization of this essential aspect of genuine thinking, the transformation of division by kind into a full-blown method or way. Working through these sections is laborious, especially in the case of the *Statesman*. We encourage our reader not to become discouraged. The reader must interrogate the stranger's divisions at each point and persist in inquiring into the basis and the unspoken implications of a given division. Only then will the dialogue yield its fruits.

Mathematics plays a key role in the *Statesman*. We know that young Socrates and Theaetetus are both students of Theodorus, and that they enjoy working on mathematical problems together (*Theaetetus* 147 C-D). Mathematics comes up at key moments in the *Statesman*. The most explicit reference occurs when the stranger suggests (by way of a joke) that human nature be defined as "the power of two" (our modern "square root of two"), meaning the power of walking on two feet (266A-B). Then there is the highly illuminating account of measurement, where the stranger takes us from a strictly mathematical kind of measurement—the determination of "how much"—to the supra-mathematical judgment of the "just right" or mean (283C-285C). Finally, the stranger's method of division itself resembles the sort of universal, teachable procedure and technique we find in mathematical studies.

Another key element is *myth*. It enters the drama because the stranger needs to clear up a confusion that occurs in one of the divisions. The myth of the *Statesman* is among the greatest in all the dialogues, and certainly the strangest. It is based on a division of cosmic time into two epochs. In one, the cosmos turns as it does now; in the other, it goes in reverse. In the former, living things sexually reproduce, grow, and die. In the latter, they spring from the earth full grown and "age" in reverse: they go from being older to being younger and eventually disappear back into the earth (270E). The cosmos continually oscillates between these two epochs. The reversed world (reversed, that is, from our perspective) is under the constant care of a benevolent and intelligent god: there is no need for cities, or politics, or a statesman. In our epoch, by contrast, the god has abandoned his guiding influence, and we are left to our own devices: political guidance is necessary. It is well beyond the scope of this Introduction to further summarize the myth: a fuller account appears in our interpretive essay. Here we confine ourselves to observing that the myth does more than correct a step in the divisions: it provides the all-embracing context, the world of gods and humans, within which statesmanship, for the stranger, is to be understood.

Paradigm is another major element. A paradigm is a guiding, authoritative example—something that can be used as a template or model. The word derives from a Greek verb that means "shows alongside of." Like myth and image, a paradigm is an indirect means of capturing a certain look, structure, or activity. The central paradigm in the *Statesman* is that of *weaving*. The stranger lavishes much attention on the technical details of this subtle female art, which seems to gather so many strands of the dialogue. Weaving is the most precise paradigm, the stranger affirms, for the statesman and the art that best mirrors statesmanly knowledge (279A-B). The statesman knows how to make a human One out of a human Many. He knows how to weave together into a sturdy and beautiful whole all the various arts and offices, and all the individuals that compose the city.

The paradigm of weaving brings us to the most striking element in the dialogue: *faction* (in Greek, *stasis*). The true statesman knows how to make a One out of a Many chiefly because he knows how to overcome faction, that is, the standing opposition between entrenched and unbudging "sides" or "parties." Political faction, for the stranger, originates in the deeper faction that exists between the forms of courage and moderation. At this advanced stage of the drama, the stranger reveals his most unconventional teaching (306B-C): that parts of virtue are not friends, as most people wrongly believe, but mutual enemies. Different individuals, whether male or female, gravitate naturally toward one or the other of these virtues. Those who tend toward courage are hard, like the solid *warp* or frame used in weaving; those who tend toward moderation are soft, like the so-called *woof*, which consists of pliant and yielding threads. Both kinds of individuals are dangerous to the city: the former in their love of war, the latter in their love of peace. Since people are attracted to their like (opposites, for the stranger, repel rather than attract), child-production only makes matters worse by perpetuating and reinforcing one-sidedness and the tendency to fanaticism.

The stranger's account of faction points to antithesis or opposition as perhaps the deepest and most interesting bond between the speech-world of the *Sophist* and the action-world of the *Statesman*. Faction is non-being as otherness at work in the realm of politics. Opposition, for the stranger, is the point at which ontology and politics meet.

Faction, more than anything else, points to statesmanship as a kind of weaving. Just as the dialectician in the realm of speech must interweave the opposed natures of Same and Other, Motion and Rest, so too the statesman in the realm of action must interweave and thereby temper the soul-extremes of "hard courageous" and "soft moderate," the warp and the woof of the political web. He makes a One out of Many through a rigorous system of education, in which noble souls overcome their one-sided virtue and become just or communal (309A-E). He intertwines extremes in the physical realm of begetting by making sure that marriage is the union of the unlike rather than the like (310A-E). Care must be taken that the rulers of cities also embody the interweaving of courage and moderation: a single ruler must unify both virtues, and a ruling group must be composed of both virtuous kinds of individuals (311A).

The discussion of faction brings us to the final definition of the statesman—or rather, as the stranger says, "the web of statesmanly action" (311B). True statesmanship is the knowledge of combining courageous and moderate natures into one all-encompassing weave. This artful act of weaving produces unanimity, friendship, and the happiness appropriate to a city. It combines in one web all the individuals in the city, both freemen and slaves, and holds them together.

Note on the Translation

As in our translations of the *Sophist* and *Phaedo*, we have tried to remain as faithful as possible to the syntax of Greek sentences, and as consistent as possible in the English rendering of the same Greek word while devising a translation that makes sense to an English speaking reader. We also tried to capture what seemed to us the right tone for what was being said by a character at any given time.

For the meanings of crucial Greek terms, the reader is encouraged to consult the Glossary that appears right after the translation. There are also two appendices: one on weaving (the central image of the *Statesman*) and another on the stranger's divisions. These may prove useful in the course of reading the dialogue.

The Greek texts used for this translation are those of John Burnet (Oxford) and H. N. Fowler (Loeb edition).

STATESMAN

Socrates
Theodorus
Stranger
Young Socrates

Socrates: I really owe you a big debt of thanks, Theodorus, 257A
for my getting to know Theaetetus, along with getting
to know the stranger as well.

Theodorus: And soon, Socrates, you'll owe triple that, once
they've worked out the statesman and the philosopher
for you.[1]

Socrates: Come now, is that how we're going to say we've
heard it put, my dear Theodorus, by the one mightiest
at calculations and geometrical matters?

Theodorus: How so, Socrates?   B

Socrates: Because you set down each of the men as of equal
worth, though in honor they stand farther apart from one
another than accords with any proportion in your art.

Theodorus: By our god Ammon, Socrates, well said and
justly—or rather your memory served you well when
you took me to task for my mistake in calculation.[2]

---

1 See *Sophist* 216C-217A. "Statesman," in Greek, is *politikos*. See Glossary
   under "city."

2 There was a famous oracle of the Egyptian god Ammon located near
   Theodorus' hometown of Cyrene in Lybia. See *Theaetetus* 143D and
   Herodotus' *Histories* I, 46 and II, 32 and 55. Theodorus' mistake is not,
   as he supposes, a mathematical one—an error in calculation—but a
   mathematician's mistake. He implicitly treats the sophist, statesman,
   and philosopher as indistinguishable monads, units of equal weight
   that can therefore have a ratio to one another.

C

Some other time, I'll get you back for this, too. But you, stranger, don't in any way tire of gratifying us, but next in order, whether you choose the statesmanly man first or the philosopher, once you've chosen, go through it.

Stranger: That, Theodorus, must be done, since, once we've taken it in hand, we mustn't leave off until we reach the end of them. But now what should I do about Theaetetus here?

Theodorus: What about him?

Stranger: Should we give him a rest and exchange him for his gym-partner, Socrates here? Or what do you advise?

Theodorus: Just as you say, make the exchange. Being young, the pair of them will easily bear every labor, if they rest by turns.

D

258A

Socrates: And besides, stranger, both risk having—from somewhere or other—a certain kinship with me. One, anyhow, appears to be like me, so you all claim, in the nature of his face, while calling and addressing the other with the same name as ours offers a certain close relation. Surely we must always be eager, I suppose, to get to know our kin through speech. Now I myself mixed it up with Theaetetus here yesterday through speech, and just now I've been listening to him answering, but I've done neither with Socrates.[3] Yet we ought to take a look at this boy, too. I'll have my turn later—for now, let him answer you.

Stranger: So it shall be. Socrates, do you hear Socrates?

Young Socrates: Yes.

Stranger: Then do you go along with what he's saying?

Young Socrates: By all means.

---

3   The "mixing it up yesterday" occurs in the *Theaetetus*. There we first learn of the striking physical resemblance between Socrates and Theaetetus (143E). The conversation that Socrates has been listening to "just now" takes place in the *Sophist*, where we first learn that Theaetetus' gym-buddy and fellow student is Socrates' namesake (218B). Speech here is *logos*, which can also mean account or argument. See Glossary under "speech."

Stranger: There appears to be nothing on your part to pre-   B
vent it, and no doubt there must be still less to prevent
it on mine. So then, after the sophist, it's necessary, as
it appears to me, for the pair of us to seek out the man
who is a statesman. And tell me whether we should
set down this man, too, as one among those who are
knowledgeable. Or how should it be?

Young Socrates: Like that.

Stranger: Then must the sciences be separated, just as when
we were looking into the man who came before?[4]

Young Socrates: Perhaps.

Stranger: Still, the cut doesn't appear to me to be along the
same lines.

Young Socrates: What then?

Stranger: Along others.   C

Young Socrates: It seems likely.

Stranger: Then where will one discover the direct states-
man-path? For we must discover it and, after separating it off from the rest, stamp it with one look,[5] and
then, after marking the other, side-paths as a single
form, make our soul think of all the sciences as being
two forms.

Young Socrates: This, I think, now turns out to be your
work, stranger, not mine.

Stranger: It must be yours, too, Socrates, whenever it be-   D
comes manifest to us.

Young Socrates: Beautifully put.

Stranger: Now aren't arithmetic, and any other arts akin to
this, stripped of actions, and don't they provide cognition only?

Young Socrates: That's so.

---

4   The "man who came before" is the sophist. The word we are translat-
ing as "science" here and elsewhere is *epistêmê*. See Glossary.

5   *idea*. See Glossary under "form."

E

Stranger: But again, the arts concerned with carpentry and every handiwork possess their science as being present within the very nature of their actions, and they bring to completion bodies arising through them that weren't there before.

Young Socrates: Certainly.

Stranger: Well then, divide all sciences together in this way, addressing one as practical, the other as cognitive only.

Young Socrates: Let there be, if you like, these as two forms of one whole science.

Stranger: Now, shall we set down the statesman and king and master, and householder too, addressing all these things as one? Or should we say that the arts themselves are as many as there are names uttered? Or rather, follow me here.

Young Socrates: Where?

259A

Stranger: Here. If someone, himself in private life, is up to advising one of the public doctors, isn't it necessary to address him by the same art-name that the one he's advising has?

Young Socrates: Yes.

Stranger: What about this? Whoever, although himself a private person, is clever enough to instruct a man who is king over a country—won't we declare him to have the science that the ruler himself must possess?

Young Socrates: We shall declare it.

B

Stranger: But surely the science that belongs to a true king is kingly?

Young Socrates: Yes.

Stranger: And won't he who possesses it, whether he happens to be a ruler or a private person, correctly be called, at least solely in accordance with the art itself, kingly?

Young Socrates: That's only just.

Stranger: And surely a householder and a master are the same thing.

Young Socrates: Of course.

Stranger: What about this? There won't be any difference with respect to rule between these two—the figure cut by a great house and again the heft of a small city, will there?

Young Socrates: None.

Stranger: Then isn't it apparent, from what we've surveyed   C
just now, that there is one science about all these things?
And whether someone names it kingly or statesmanly
or householding, let's not differ with him.

Young Socrates: Why should we?

Stranger: But surely this too is plain, that any king at all has very little power in his hands, and in all his body together, to hold onto his rule, compared with the understanding and strength of his soul.

Young Socrates: That's plain.

Stranger: Then do you want us to declare that the king is more closely related to the cognitive art than to handi-   D
craft or the practical generally?

Young Socrates: Of course.

Stranger: Then the statesmanly art and statesman, and kingly art and kingly man—shall we put all these together in the same group, as being all one?

Young Socrates: That's plain.

Stranger: Then wouldn't we be proceeding in order if, after this, we were to delimit the cognitive art?

Young Socrates: Entirely so.

Stranger: Now apply your mind to this: whether we can in fact perceive any natural cleft in it.

Young Socrates: Say what sort.

E   **Stranger:** This sort. I suppose, in our view, there's a certain art of number-reasoning—[6]

Young Socrates: Yes.

Stranger: —belonging, I think, altogether to the cognitive arts.

Young Socrates: Of course.

Stranger: And when number-reasoning has cognized the difference among numbers, shall we give it any further work than to judge the things cognized?

Young Socrates: Of course not.

Stranger: And surely every master-builder is not himself at work but is a master of workmen—

Young Socrates: Yes.

Stranger: —somehow furnishing cognition but not handiwork.

Young Socrates: That's so.

260A   **Stranger:** Then he might justly be said to partake of cognitive science.[7]

Young Socrates: Entirely so.

Stranger: But I suppose it's fitting for this man, once he's made a judgment, not to be finished—not to be done with it, the way the number-reasoner was done—but to prescribe what's suitable to each of the workers, until they've worked out what was prescribed.

Young Socrates: Correct.

Stranger: Then are all such sciences, and so many as follow along with number-reasoning, together cognitive—

---

6   *logistikê.* See Glossary under "arithmetic." In the *Gorgias* Socrates distinguishes between logistic or number-reasoning and arithmetic: both sciences deal with the odd and the even, but they differ in that "logistic looks into the even and the odd with respect to the multitude they make in relation both to themselves and to one another" (451B-C). For a fuller account of *logistikê,* see Jacob Klein, *Greek Mathematical Thought and the Origin of Algebra* (Cambridge: M. I. T. Press, 1968), pp. 17-25.

7   Not to be confused, of course, with the contemporary meaning of the term.

while these kinds as a pair differ from each other with   B
respect to judging and commanding?

Young Socrates: They appear to.

Stranger: Then if, in dividing, we were to call one part of
cognitive science as a whole "commanding," the other
"judging," might we claim to have divided elegantly?

Young Socrates: In my opinion at least.

Stranger: But surely for those who are doing something in
common, it's desirable to be of one mind.

Young Socrates: Of course.

Stranger: Then so long as we alone have this in common ourselves, we shall bid farewell to the opinions of others.

Young Socrates: Certainly.

Stranger: Proceed then. In which of these two arts must we   C
put the kingly man? In the judging art, as if he were
some spectator? Or shall we rather put him down as
belonging to the commanding art, since he masters?

Young Socrates: Why, in the latter, of course.

Stranger: Then as for the commanding art, it would be again
necessary to see if there's a separation in it somewhere.
And I think it's right here: Just as the art of retailers
is distinguished from the art of self-sellers, so too the   D
kingly kind seems to be bounded off from the herald-
kind.

Young Socrates: How so?

Stranger: Retailers first receive, then sell again for a second
time, the works of others, which, I suppose, have been
sold before.

Young Socrates: By all means.

Stranger: And so, the heralding tribe, once it receives thoughts commanded by others, itself gives the commands, a second time, to others.

Young Socrates: Most true.

E

Stranger: What then? Shall we mix the kingly art into the same group with that of the interpreter, the boatswain, the prophet, the herald, and many other arts akin to these, all having to do with commanding? Or, if you wish, just as we were making a likeness a moment ago, should we make a parallel likeness in name too, since the kind of those who give their own commands happens to be pretty much nameless? And shall we divide these things in this way: put the king-kind in the art of "self-commanding" and, since we don't care about all the rest, leave room for someone to set down another name for them? For our pursuit was for the sake of the

261A   ruler, not his opposite.

Young Socrates: By all means.

Stranger: So then, since this group stands fairly distant from them, distinguished by other-ness as opposed to own-ness, isn't it necessary to divide this very one in its turn, if we still have some place within it that yields to our cut?

Young Socrates: Entirely so.

Stranger: And indeed, we appear to have one—but follow along and make the cut with me.

Young Socrates: Where?

B

Stranger: All those rulers we notice making use of commands—won't we find them giving prescriptions for the sake of some generating?

Young Socrates: How could this not be?

Stranger: And surely it's not difficult to separate all the things that are generated into two groups.

Young Socrates: In what way?

Stranger: Of all of them taken together, some, I suppose, are soulless, others ensouled.

Young Socrates: Yes.

Stranger: And if in fact we want to cut the part of the cognitive that commands, we'll cut it along the very same lines.

Young Socrates: Along which lines?

Stranger: By ordaining part of it for the generating of soulless things, part for that of ensouled things. And in this way all will be at once divided in two.   C

Young Socrates: Altogether so.

Stranger: Well then, let's leave aside one of them and take up the other; and once we've taken it up, let's partition the whole of it in two.

Young Socrates: And you're saying we must take up which of the two?

Stranger: Surely the part that gives commands concerning animals. The part that belongs to kingly science is certainly never in charge of soulless things, as if it were the job of a master builder, but is better born, always possessing its power among animals and concerning   D just these.

Young Socrates: Correct.

Stranger: At least regarding the generating and nurture of animals, one might see one sort as single-nurturing, the other as the collective care for creatures in herds.

Young Socrates: Correct.

Stranger: But surely we won't find the statesman to be a private-nurturer, like an ox-driver or some sort of horse-groom, but more like a horse-feeder or cattle-feeder.

Young Socrates: What's been said just now at least appears true.

Stranger: So are we naming the sort of animal-nurture that's   E the collective nurture of many animals *herd-nurture* or a sort of *collective-nurture art*?

Young Socrates: Whichever falls out in the argument.

Stranger: Beautiful, Socrates. And if you guard against being serious about names, you'll show yourself richer in intelligence in old age. And now, just what you bid must be done. But regarding the herd-nurturing art, do you see where someone who's shown it to be double will make what's now sought among twice as many then be sought among half?

262A

Young Socrates: I'll put my heart into it. And so it seems to me that there is one distinct nurture of humans, another again of beasts.

Stranger: You've divided altogether most heartily and manfully. Let's not, however, have this happen to us once again, if it's in our power—

Young Socrates: What?

Stranger: Let's not divide off one small portion in opposition to many big things, nor apart from a form. Instead, let the part have a form as well. For it's all very fine to separate straightaway the thing sought from the others, if it's done correctly. In the same way, just a little while ago, you thought you had the division and pressed on with the argument, because you saw it making its way toward human beings. But really, my friend, it's not safe to make small change: it's safer to proceed by cutting through middles, and one might be more apt to come upon looks. And this makes all the difference in inquiries.

B

C

Young Socrates: What do you mean by that, stranger?

Stranger: An attempt must be made, Socrates, to state the matter yet more clearly, out of good will toward your nature. Now at the present moment, however, it's impossible to make plain what's now at issue without falling short. But we must endeavor to advance the matter a little more amply for the sake of lucidity further on.

Young Socrates: What sort of thing, then, do you declare we did incorrectly in our dividing just now?

Stranger: This sort. It's as if someone attempting to divide humankind into two were to divide it just as most people here distribute it. On the one hand, they divide off and separate the Hellenic kind from all others as being one; and on the other, by applying one appellation—"barbarian"—to all the other kinds, which are unlimited and unmixable and dissonant with each other, they expect this something, just because of this one appellation, to be one kind as well. Or again, it's if someone were to consider that he was dividing number according to two forms by cutting off the first ten-thousand from all the other numbers, as though separating off one form, and putting one name on all the rest, and if he should then, by reason of this appellation, think it fit for this kind too to be apart from the former and so to be another single form. He would, I suppose, divide more beautifully, and rather more according to forms and in two, if he were to cut number into even and odd, and, again, humankind into male and female; but Lydians or Phrygians or whatever others he marshaled against all the rest he would split off only when he was at an impasse about finding each of the groups that resulted from the split to be a kind as well as a part.

Young Socrates: Most correct. But that's just it, stranger. How might one recognize kind and part more distinctly, and see that the two are not the same thing but different from one another?

Stranger: You best of men, Socrates, it's no mean task you're prescribing. We've recently wandered farther from the proposed account than was necessary, and you're urging us to wander even more. So for now, let's go back again, as is fitting; and some other time, at our leisure, we'll go after that other thing, just like trackers. Only by all means guard against thinking the following: that you ever heard it distinctly ordained by me—

Young Socrates: What?

Stranger: —that form and part are other than one another.

Young Socrates: So what *are* you saying?

Stranger: That whenever there's a form of anything, it's necessary that it also be part of the thing of whatever it is said to be a form; but there's no necessity that part be form. Always declare, Socrates, that I say it this way rather than that other way.

Young Socrates: It will be done.

C **Stranger:** Then attend to this next point for me.

Young Socrates: Which one?

Stranger: That point of our wandering off that led us here. For I think it was the moment when, asked in what way herd-nurturing should be divided, you really put your heart into saying that there were two kinds of animals: one the human kind, the other a single kind of all the other beasts taken together.

Young Socrates: True.

Stranger: And to me at any rate you appeared at that time to think that in taking away a part you left behind what remains as a single kind, because you were able to name them all by the same name, having called them beasts.

D

Young Socrates: That's how it was all right.

Stranger: But indeed, you most courageous of all men, perhaps if there's some other animal somewhere that's intelligent, such as the crane-kind seems to be, or some other such kind, which perhaps distinguishes by names along the same lines as you do, it might oppose cranes as one kind to other animals and on its own give itself airs and, lumping all the rest together into the same group, along with humans, address them as nothing other, perhaps, than beasts. So let's try to be very cautious about all such things of that sort.

E **Young Socrates:** How?

Stranger: By not dividing the whole animal-kind, in order to be less prone to such afflictions.

Young Socrates: We shouldn't.

Stranger: No, for it was exactly in that way that an error was made earlier.

Young Socrates: What was that?

Stranger: All the command-giving part of cognitive science that concerned us had to do, I suppose, with the animal-nurturing kind—though, to be sure, of herd-animals. Wasn't that so?

Young Socrates: Yes.

Stranger: So then, the whole of what's alive was divided even then into domesticated and wild. For animals that have a nature suited to domestication are addressed as tame, those that are not willing, as wild.

264A

Young Socrates: Beautiful.

Stranger: But at least the science we're hunting was and is to be sought among tame creatures, in fact, among creatures in herds.

Young Socrates: Yes.

Stranger: So then, let's not divide as we did earlier when we fixed our gaze on all animals, nor rush in order to come quickly to statesmanship. For even now, that's made us suffer the proverbial affliction.

B

Young Socrates: What's that?

Stranger: By not dividing well and calmly, to have hastened only to go more slowly.

Young Socrates: And a fine thing that it did make us do so, stranger.

Stranger: So be it. Once again, then, from the beginning, let's try to divide the art of collective nurture. For perhaps the argument itself, as it comes to a conclusion, will disclose to you rather beautifully even the very thing you're eager for. And tell me—

Young Socrates: What exactly?

Stranger: Just this, if you've perhaps heard it from certain people—for I know you haven't yourself encountered the tamed among the fish of the Nile and those in the

C

ponds of the Great King.[8] Still, I suppose you might've seen them in fountain pools.

Young Socrates: By all means, I've both seen the latter and have heard of the former from many people.

Stranger: And surely, even if you haven't wandered around the Thessalian plains, you've at any rate heard there are, and believe there exist, goose-nurseries and crane-nurseries.

Young Socrates: Certainly.

D **Stranger:** I asked you all these things for this reason: Of the nurture of herds, there's a part that's water-immersed, but there's also a dry-land-based part.

Young Socrates: That's so.

Stranger: Then does it seem to you as well that we must split the science of collective nurture in two, assigning a part of the science to each of these two by naming one part wet-nurture, the other dry-land-nurture?

Young Socrates: It seems so to me.

Stranger: And surely we won't search for which art king-
E ship belongs to, for it's plain to everyone.

Young Socrates: Of course.

Stranger: Now everyone could divide the land-nurture breed of herd-nurture.

Young Socrates: How?

Stranger: By marking it off into the winged and the footed.

Young Socrates: Most true.

Stranger: What about this? Surely what pertains to states-manship must be sought in the realm of the footed, mustn't it? Or don't you suppose that even, so to speak, the most thoughtless person will think this way?

Young Socrates: I do.

---

8   The Great King is the king of Persia, Artaxerxes II at the time of this conversation—399 B.C., the year of Socrates' execution.

Stranger: But we must display the footed-pasturing art as cut in two, just like an even number.

Young Socrates: That's plain.

Stranger: And surely our account has set off toward those 265A parts where it appears to catch sight of a certain two-some, a pair of ways stretching out. The one way is quicker, dividing off into a small part relative to a big one; the other—keeping rather to what we said in what went before, that we must cut in the middle as much as we can—is indeed longer. So it's possible for us to pass along whichever way we wish.

Young Socrates: What about this—is it impossible to go by both?

Stranger: By both at once, indeed, wonder-boy! But to go in turn, yes, it's plain enough that it's possible.

Young Socrates: Then I, for one, choose both in turn.   B

Stranger: That's easy, since what's left is brief. At the beginning surely, and also at the middle stages of the passage, the assignment would have been hard for us. But now, since this seems right, let's go by the longer one first. For we'll pass along it more easily, since we're fresher.

Young Socrates: Speak.

Stranger: The footed among our tame animals, as many as live in herds, are by nature divided in two.

Young Socrates: In what way?

Stranger: By the fact that some are by generation hornless, others horn-bearing.

Young Socrates: So it appears.   C

Stranger: Now once you've divided the footed-pasturing art, hand it over, one to each of two parts, using description. For if you wanted to name them, it will be more intricately intertwined for you than is necessary.

Young Socrates: Then how should one speak?

Stranger: Like this. When the footed-pasturing science has been divided in two, one sub-part is assigned to the horn-bearing, the other to the hornless part of the herd.

Young Socrates: Let that be said, and in this way, for it's
been made entirely and sufficiently plain.

D

Stranger: And moreover, the king at least is manifest to us
as one who pastures a certain horn-shorn herd.

Young Socrates: How could he not be plain?

Stranger: Let us therefore try, by breaking down this herd,
to hand over to him what proves to be his.

Young Socrates: Entirely so.

Stranger: The question is whether you want to divide it according to "cloven" and so-called "mono-hoof," or
according to "crossbreeding" and "own-breeding." I
suppose you understand—

Young Socrates: What?

E

Stranger: —that horses and asses by nature breed from each
other.

Young Socrates: Yes.

Stranger: While what still remains of the smooth herd of
tame animals is unmixed in kind, one with the other.

Young Socrates: Of course.

Stranger: What about this? The statesman appears to have
care of which of these: the crossbreeding or a certain
own-breeding nature?

Young Socrates: It's plain that it's of the unmixed one.

Stranger: This one, it surely seems, we must lay out in two,
just as before.

Young Socrates: Yes, we must.

266A

Stranger: And surely animal, as much of it as is tame and
in herds, has all been pretty much already sliced up,
except for a pair of kinds; for the dog-kind isn't worthy
of being numbered as among herd creatures.

Young Socrates: No, it isn't. But in what way exactly are we
dividing the pair?

Stranger: In the very way that it's also just for both you and

Theaetetus to distribute them, since you both grasp geometry.

Young Socrates: Which way is that?

Stranger: By the diagonal, of course, and again by the diagonal of the square on the diagonal.[9]

Young Socrates: What are you saying?

Stranger: The nature that our human-kind possesses—is it naturally related to walking in any way other than just like the diagonal that's two feet in power?   B

Young Socrates: Nothing else.

Stranger: And surely the nature of the remaining kind is, again, according to power, the diagonal of the square constructed on our power, if in fact it's the nature of twice a pair of feet.

Young Socrates: Of course, it is. And what's more, I pretty much understand what you want to make plain.

Stranger: Indeed, in addition to this, Socrates, do we see that a second thing has also come about in our divisions, something that could gain reputation as a joke?   C

Young Socrates: What sort of thing?

Stranger: Our human kind, having together shared the same lot and run in the same race with the kind which, among beings, is the most well-bred and also the easiest to manage.

---

9   "Diagonal" is *diametros* or diameter, the line that divides a square into two right triangles. In the unit square, whose area is one square foot, the diagonal has a length equal to (in modern terms) the square root of two. The length of the diagonal of the square constructed on this line is two. This diagonal is "the diagonal of the square on the diagonal." In the *Meno* Socrates shows the slave-boy that the square whose area is double that of a given square is constructed on the diagonal of that square (82B ff.). The diagonal of the unit square was sometimes called "the diameter that is two feet in power" (*hê diametros hê dynamei dipous*), where power, *dynamis*, refers to a square root (see Glossary under "power"). The stranger introduces these mathematical terms to set up his wordplay on "our power" of two feet, which appears just below. In the dialogue that bears his name, Theaetetus rallies all the separate *dynameis* or "roots" in a single definition (147D-148B). For pictures of the stranger's squares, see note 8 of the Essay.

Young Socrates: I see this coming about very strangely, too.

Stranger: But what other result could there have been? Isn't it likely for the slowest to have arrived latest?[10]

Young Socrates: Yes, that's so.

Stranger: And don't we notice this: that the king appears still more laughable, running around with the herd and having kept up in the race with the one among men who for his part is the most excellently trained for an easily managed life?[11]

D

Young Socrates: Entirely so.

Stranger: For now, Socrates, that statement uttered earlier in our search regarding the sophist is especially manifest.

Young Socrates: Which one?

Stranger: That in this sort of pursuit of accounts, there was no care for what was dignified any more than for what wasn't, and it didn't dishonor the small in favor of the great, but on its own terms always reaches what is most true.[12]

Young Socrates: So it seems.

Stranger: Then after this, in order that you not anticipate me with a question, should I myself go the shorter way for you, the one mentioned earlier, which leads to the distinguishing mark of the king?

E

---

10 The "the most well-bred and also the easiest to manage" animal is the pig. The stranger now plays on the resemblance between *hys* (pig) and *hystaton* (last or latest).

11 The pairing of men and pigs, and the king and the swineherd, recalls Odysseus' faithful swineherd, Eumaeus, whom Homer calls "leader of men" (*Odyssey* XIV, 22). One also thinks of Circe, who turned Odysseus' men into pigs (X, 233 ff.).

12 In the *Sophist*, the stranger asserts that his *methodos tôn logôn*—his way or pursuit of accounts—honors all the arts equally, including those of the general and the louse-catcher (227A-C).

Young Socrates: Very much so.

Stranger: I say, then, that earlier, one should have distributed the footed kind immediately into the two-footed as against the four-footed, and, having in view that the human kind has continued to share the same fate only with the winged kind, one should again cut the two-footed herd into the naked and the feather-natured kind; and once it was cut and the human-pasturing art was already made plain at that point, taking the statesmanly and kingly man and placing him in it as a sort of charioteer, one should hand over to him the reins of the city, since these are proper to him and this is his science.

Young Socrates: Beautifully you've set the account straight for me and, as if paying a debt, added on the digression and filled out the account, as if with interest.

267A

Stranger: Come then. Once we've gone back to the beginning, let's string together the account of the name of the statesman's art right to the end.

Young Socrates: By all means.

Stranger: Well then, to begin with, commanding was for us a part of cognitive science; and the portion of this, developed by way of a likeness, was called "self-commanding." And again, animal-nurturing science was split off as not the least of the kinds of self-commanding science; and a herd-nurturing form from animal-nurturing science, and in turn a footed-pasturing form from herd-nurturing. And from the footed-pasturing form was cut off in particular an art that nurtures the hornless nature. And of this art in turn it's necessary—should someone wish to bring it together under one name—to weave together a part that's not less than threefold, by addressing it as a "science" of "pasturing" an "unmixed breed." And the cut from the latter, since a human-pasturing part is the only thing still left for the two-footed flock—this is just what has now been sought, the same thing called at once kingly and statesmanly.

B

C

Young Socrates: Altogether so.

Stranger: But Socrates, has this indeed been truly accomplished for us in the way you put it just now?

Young Socrates: What, exactly?

Stranger: That the thing proposed has been articulated altogether sufficiently. Or does the search most certainly fall short in just this way—the account has in some sense been articulated but has not been completely worked out.

D

Young Socrates: How do you mean?

Stranger: I'll try to do just this for the two of us, to make what I'm thinking of now still more plain.

Young Socrates: Please speak.

Stranger: Now of the many arts of pasturing that came to sight for us just now, one of them in particular was statesmanship, and it was the care for one particular herd?

Young Socrates: Yes.

Stranger: And this art the account marked off as the nurture, not of horses or other beasts, but as the science of the collective nurture of human beings.

Young Socrates: Just so.

E

Stranger: Let's observe this very difference between all herdsmen and kings.

Young Socrates: Which one?

Stranger: Whether in the case of the other herdsmen, there's someone—with the name of a different art—who claims to be and pretends to be in common a fellow-nurturer of the herd.

Young Socrates: How do you mean?

Stranger: Take traders and farmers and millers all, and in addition sports trainers and the doctor-kind—do you know that all these together would in every way

268A   do battle in speech with those engaged in pasturing human stock, the ones we called statesmen, on the grounds that they themselves take care of human nurture, not only of herd-humans but even of the nurture of the rulers themselves?

Young Socrates: Wouldn't they say so correctly?

Stranger: Perhaps. And we'll look into that, but this we know, that nobody will dispute with a cowherd about any of these matters, but the cowman himself is the nurturer of his herd, himself the doctor, himself the matchmaker, as it were, and he alone is knowledgeable in the art of midwifery, which is concerned with the deliveries and childbirths of the newborns. Furthermore, to whatever degree his creatures participate by nature in play and music, nobody else is superior at appeasing and, by beguiling, gentling them; either with instruments or by solo voice, he best employs the music suited to his flock. And so too, other herd-pasturers behave in the same manner. Don't they?

Young Socrates: Most correct.

Stranger: How, then, will our account, the one about the king, appear correct and undiluted when we posit him alone as herdsman and nurturer of the human herd, selecting him from among thousands of others who dispute the claim?

Young Socrates: There's no way it can.

Stranger: Then weren't we correctly afraid a little before when we suspected that we might indeed have happened to be describing a certain kingly shape but somehow might not have worked out the statesman with precision until, having stripped off those who clung around him and made counterclaims to joint pasturing with him, and, having separated him from those people, we displayed him pure, alone?

Young Socrates: That's certainly most correct.

Stranger: Then we must do this, Socrates, if we're not to disgrace our account at the end.

Young Socrates: But surely there's no way we should do that!

Stranger: Then we must go back and, from a different beginning, make our passage along some other way.

Young Socrates: Which way is that?

Stranger: Diluting it with something close to play; for we must make use of a long part of a great story, and, for the remainder, do just as before—always taking away part from part to arrive, at the peak, at what is sought. Isn't that what's wanted?

E

Young Socrates: By all means.

Stranger: But apply your mind entirely to my story, just as children do; at all events, you're not quit of children's games by that many years.

Young Socrates: Please tell it.

Stranger: Now there happened, and will yet happen, many of the other matters anciently recounted, and so also the omen concerning the recounted quarrel between Atreus and Thyestes. You've probably heard and remember what they say came to pass then.

Young Socrates: Are you perhaps referring to the sign of the golden lamb?

269A **Stranger:** Not at all, but rather to the one about the change in both the setting and the rising of the sun, and of the other heavenly bodies—how at that time they used to set in that region where they now rise, and used to rise in the opposite region; but then the god, in testimony on behalf of Atreus, changed it to the scheme we have now.[13]

Young Socrates: That, too, is certainly what they say.

---

13   In his play *Orestes* (988 ff.), Euripides tells the story that connects these three elements: the quarrel between Atreus and Thyestes, the sign of the golden lamb, and the change in the setting and rising of the sun. There was a curse on the house of Atreus. A baleful portent, a lamb with a golden fleece that appeared in Atreus' flocks, signified his right to rule Argos. Thyestes, however, took the lamb and the crown. To vindicate Atreus, Zeus reversed the course of the sun. The infamous banquet, at which Atreus served Thyestes the latter's own children's flesh, was a consequence of their quarrel.

Stranger: And again, we've often heard about the kingdom that Cronos ruled.[14]

Young Socrates: Indeed, very often.

B

Stranger: And what about this story, that those who lived in olden days were by nature earth-born and not generated from each other?[15]

Young Socrates: That, too, is one of the things anciently recounted.

Stranger: Well then, all these stories taken together—and thousands of others in addition still more wondrous than these—come from the same disturbance; but through a great lapse of time some of them have died out, while others, having been scattered about, are each told separate from the others. But as for the disturbance that is the cause of all these things, no one has told of it, and that's exactly what must now be recounted, for once uttered it will be fitting for the showing-forth of the king.

C

Young Socrates: Most beautifully put—and tell it, leaving nothing out.

Stranger: Please listen. At one time the god himself accompanies this all as guide and helps it in its circling as it makes its way; at another he lets it go, whenever the cycles have now reached the measure of the time suited to the cosmos, and then it rotates of its own accord backwards in the opposite direction, since it is an animal and has been allotted intelligence from the one who joined it together in the beginning. And this going in reverse is by necessity naturally ingrained in it for the following reason.

D

Young Socrates: What reason is that?

---

14 Hesiod, in his epic poem *Works and Days* (110 ff.), tells how the gods made a golden race of men when Cronus was king in heaven. These lived free from toil, pain, and miserable old age; and the earth, unforced, bore them abundant fruit.

15 Hesiod, in his epic poem the *Theogony* (154 ff.), tells how the Giants were born of Earth (Gaia) and the blood of Heaven (Ouranos), which fell on the earth when he was castrated by his son Cronus at the behest of Gaia.

Stranger: Always holding to the self-same and similar condition and always being the same befits only the most divine of all things, and the nature of body is not of this rank.

E

And what we've named heaven and cosmos has participated in many blessed things from its begetter, but even so it also communes with body; whence it is impossible for it to be entirely without a share in change, however much it moves (at least insofar as it's able) with a single sweep in the same spot and in the same way; therefore, it has taken back-circling as its lot, because this is the smallest deviation from the motion that is its own. But it's hardly possible for anything by itself to turn itself always, except for that which leads all the things that move; and for this to produce motion alternately, now in one direction and again in the opposite direction, is forbidden. And so, as a consequence of all this, one should declare neither that the cosmos on its own always turns itself, nor again that it is always turned as a whole by god in two, and opposite, rotations, nor yet again that some pair of opposite-minded gods turn it, but instead, the very thing that was said just now and that alone remains: at one time it is accompanied by a different divine cause as guide, as it acquires life again and takes on repaired immortality from the craftsman; and then, whenever it's let go, it goes on its own through itself, released at just such a moment as to make its way backwards through many thousands of cycles, for the very reason that, though it's the biggest thing, it goes in the most equally balanced way as it travels upon the smallest foot.

270A

B

Young Socrates: Everything you've gone through at least appears to have been put very reasonably.

Stranger: So on the basis of what's now been said, let's figure out and reflect on the disturbance that we declared was responsible for all these wondrous things. It's in fact just this.

Young Socrates: What?

Stranger: That the sweep of the all is swept around at one time in the direction it now circles in, at another in the opposite direction.

Young Socrates: How's that?

Stranger: This change, of all the turnings that arise with regard to the heavens, we're bound to regard as the greatest and most complete turning.   C

Young Socrates: That seems likely, at any rate.

Stranger: Well then, one should also think that for those of us who dwell within the heavens the greatest changes come to pass at that time.

Young Socrates: This, too, seems likely.

Stranger: And don't we know that the nature of animals endures with difficulty, when changes great and many and various bear down on it?

Young Socrates: Of course.

Stranger: Well then, there occur at that time, of necessity, the greatest destructions of the rest of the animals, and in particular only some small remnant of humanity is left   D
behind. And different afflictions, many and wondrous and strange, befall these men, but this one is greatest, and it goes along with the back-spinning of the all that occurs at that time, when the turning that's opposed to what's now established comes to pass.

Young Socrates: Which one?

Stranger: First, the age that each of the animals had currently reached stood still for all of them, and every being that was mortal stopped its progression toward looking older. And then, changing to the opposite di-   E
rection, it grew, as it were, younger and more tender. And the white hair of the older ones grew black, and the cheeks of those with beards, as they grew smooth again, restored each to its bygone prime. And the bodies of those who were young, in growing smooth and becoming smaller with each day and each night, regressed to the nature of a newborn child, becoming like it in both soul and body; and from then on, already withering away, they disappeared completely and utterly. And as for those in turn who came to a violent end at that time, the body of the dead man, after un-

dergoing these same afflictions swiftly, wasted away in a few days and vanished.

271A **Young Socrates:** But the generation of animals at that time, stranger—what was that exactly? And in what manner were they begotten from one another?

Stranger: It's plain, Socrates, that being begotten from one another was not in the nature of things back then. But rather the earthborn kind said to have once existed[16] was at that time turned back up out of the earth and was so remembered by our first forefathers, who were

B neighbors in the time adjacent to that earlier circuit, as it was ending, and had sprung up at the beginning of this one. For these became the heralds to us of those accounts that are now disbelieved by many, but not correctly. One should, I think, reflect on what came from this. For it follows from the going back of the old ones to the nature of the child that they were recomposed and revived anew there out of those who had died and were lying in the earth, since, as a result of the turn, generation had circled back to its opposite. And so, according to this account, they, from necessity, sprang

C up earthborn; and that's how they got the name and the account—at least as many of them as the gods did not reserve for another fate.[17]

Young Socrates: Yes, that's exactly what follows from what went before. But that life that you claim is under the sway of Cronos—was it in those turnings or in these? For plainly it falls out that change in the course of the stars and the sun happens in either set of turnings.

Stranger: You have followed along with the account beauti-
D fully. What you were asking about—when everything came about of itself for human beings—doesn't in the least belong to the now-established sweep of things,

---

16 These are not the Giants of note 15 but ordinary humans in the Age of Cronos.

17 Hesiod, in *Works and Days* (167-73), says that before present mankind, Zeus had made another god-like race of hero-men, some of whom were enshrouded by death before Thebes and Troy, while others received from him a life untouched by sorrows on the Isles of the Blessed at the ends of the earth.

but it too was part of the one before. To begin with, god at that time ruled the circling itself, caring for the whole of it. And so, in the same way, all the parts of the cosmos were in their turn divided according to regions under gods who ruled them. Moreover, spirits, like divine herdsmen, separated the animals according to kinds and herds, each spirit being in all things self-sufficient in respect to each of those he himself was E pasturing, so that no animal was wild or fodder for another, and there was no war among them nor any faction at all. But whatever else follows from such a cosmic ordering would take a thousand words to tell. So then, what was said about humans, that their life came about of itself, was uttered for some such reason as the following. God himself as overseer was pasturing them, just as humans do now, who, being a different and more divine animal, pasture other kinds inferior to themselves. But when that one had the pasturing, there were no regimes, and no possession of women and children, for out of the earth they all 272A came back to life again, remembering nothing of what happened before. But all such things were absent, and they always had bounteous fruits from trees and from many various bushes, fruits that always sprouted not by agriculture but by the earth, which of itself yielded them. And they used to dwell mostly out of doors, naked and without bedding, for the seasons had been blended to be harmless for them, and for soft beds they had the grass that sprouted up from the ungrudging earth. What you are hearing, Socrates, is the life of B those in the time of Cronos, while this life, our current one, which is accounted to be in the time of Zeus, you are around to perceive for yourself. And would you be able, and also willing, to judge which of the pair of lives is happier?

Young Socrates: Not at all.

Stranger: Then do you want me, in some manner, to render you a judgment?

Young Socrates: By all means.

Stranger: Well then, if the foster-children of Cronos, with

that much leisure attending them and the possibility
of being able to engage in conversations not only with
C   humans but also with beasts, made full use of all these
advantages for the purpose of philosophy, by associ-
ating both with beasts and with one another, and by
learning from every nature whether one of them that
has some special power has perceived something dis-
tinctive that set it apart from the others and contrib-
uted to the gathering of intelligence, then it's easy to
judge that the people back then excelled a thousand-
fold those of the present in point of happiness. But if,
when filled up with a surfeit of food and drink, they
told each other and the beasts the sort of stories that
D   are told even now about them, then this too, to declare
it according to my opinion at least, is also very easy to
judge. However, let's hold off from these things until some informer appears who is up to telling us in
which of the two ways people back then had desires
regarding both sciences and the use of accounts. As
for the purpose for which we revived the story, this
must be uttered, in order that afterwards we may forge
ahead to a finish. For when the time of all these events
had reached its end and the change had to take place,
E   and when, moreover, the entire earthy kind had already been spent, since each soul had given up all her
generations, having fallen into the ground as seed as
many times as had been ordained for each, at that very
moment the helmsman of the all, having released the
handle of the rudder, withdrew to his lookout point,
while both destiny and inborn desire turned the cosmos back again. Then all the gods who in their several
regions rule together with the supreme spirit, having
recognized at once what was happening, released in
turn the parts of the cosmos from their care.

273A   And the cosmos reversed itself and crashed, having set
off an impulse where beginning and end are at odds,
and it made a great earthquake within itself and so
again produced another destruction of all sorts of animals. And after this, when enough time had gone by,
it now ceased from tumults and confusion, obtained
calm after the earthquakes and entered in an orderly

way into its habitual course, itself exercising care and
control both over the things within itself and over it-   B
self, and remembering the teaching of its craftsman
and father as best it could. Now at the beginning it
used to accomplish its end more precisely, but in the
end more dully. And the mixture's bodily aspect—
fellow-nursling of primeval nature—is responsible
for all these things in it, since it participated in much
disarray before arriving at the present cosmic order.
For from its composer the cosmos has acquired all that
is beautiful; but from its previous condition—out of
that—the cosmos itself possesses and produces among
the animals everything under the heavens that turns   C
out to be harsh and unjust. So then, while the cosmos
nourishes the animals, with the aid of its pilot, it brings
forth small evils and great goods within itself. But once
it is separated from him, it always manages all things
most beautifully during the time that's closest to its
point of release; but as time goes on and forgetfulness
arises within it, the condition of ancient disharmony
also holds sway with it more and more, and as the time   D
approaches its end, the cosmos yields small goods, and
administering to itself a great mixture of opposites, it
reaches the point of risking destruction both of itself
and of the things within it. And so, at just this moment,
the god who had put it in order, seeing the cosmos at
an impasse and concerned that it not—tempest-tossed
and shattered by confusion—plunge into the boundless sea of unlikeness, once again takes his seat at the   E
helm; and after turning around what was sick and
slack within the earlier cycle when the cosmos was on
its own, he puts it in order and, in setting it upright
again, fashions it into something immortal and ageless.

Now with this we've reached the end-point of everything we were saying; but as for the showing-forth of
the king, it's enough for us to latch onto the account at
an earlier point. For when the cosmos was turned once
more into the way that leads toward generation as it is
now, aging once again came to a standstill and yielded
new things that were the opposite of what happened
before. Animals that fell little short of disappearing

as a result of smallness started growing, while bodies new-born from the earth, having grown gray and dying again, went down into the earth. And all the other

274A things also changed, imitating and following along with the condition of the all, and so too did pregnancy and birth and nourishment, in their imitation, follow along with all the other things by necessity; for it was no longer possible for any animal to grow in the earth by composition from other things, but just as it was prescribed for the cosmos to be the self-ruler of its own passage, so too in the same way it had been prescribed for the parts themselves to grow and beget and nourish, through themselves as far as was possible, under the same dispensation.

B   Now, at last, we are at the point for the sake of which the whole account started off. There would be much to go through, and at length, about the other beasts: from what and through which causes each had changed. About humans, however, the account is briefer and more relevant. For since they were bereft of the care of the spirit who had possessed and pastured us, and since, moreover, most of the beasts—those who were harsh in their natures—had grown wild, humans themselves, having become weak and unprotected, were savaged by them; and, what's more, they were

C   in those first years still without contrivances and arts, inasmuch as nourishment that came of itself had given out, and they were not yet knowledgeable about how to provide for themselves, because hitherto no need had made it necessary for them. For all these reasons they were in great straits.

Wherefore the storied gifts of old were given to us by gods, together with necessary education and upbring-

D   ing: fire from Prometheus, arts from Hephaestus and his fellow-artisan, and seeds as well as plants from oth-

ers.[18] And all things whatever that have helped to set
up human life have come from them, since, as was said
just now, the condition of care from the gods had given
out, and humans themselves needed to take hold of
the course of their lives and its care on their own, just
like the whole cosmos, with which we, imitating and
following along with it, through time everlasting, live
and grow now in this way, now in that. And so, let this   E
indeed be the end of the story, but we will make it useful for discerning how far off the mark we were when
we expounded the kingly and statesmanly man in the
previous account.

Young Socrates: How, then, did we miss the mark—and
how great an error do you claim we made?

Stranger: In one way it was rather negligible, in another
more genuine and a lot greater and more far-reaching
than I claimed earlier.

Young Socrates: How?

Stranger: In that, when we were asked for the king and
statesman of the present cycle and generation, we were
speaking of the shepherd of the human herd *then* who   275A
belonged to the opposite turning and was accordingly
a god rather than a mortal—in this we went very, very
much astray. But because we declared him to be the
ruler of his entire city, and didn't fully make manifest
in what manner he ruled, in this respect what we said
was true, yet it surely was uttered in a way that was
not whole, nor clear, which is why the error we made
was more negligible than the other one.

Young Socrates: True.

Stranger: Then we must expect the statesman, as it seems, to
have been perfectly articulated by us in this way—only
after we've marked off the manner of his rule of the city.

---

18   Hesiod, in his *Theogony* (562 ff.), tells the story of Prometheus ("Fore-
thinker"), who, hiding Zeus' fire in a fennel stalk, stole it and gave it
to humans against the god's will. Hephaestus was the divine craftsman, a lame smith-god and an artist, who was on especially friendly
terms with Athena, the goddess of Athens, who patronized the arts
and crafts, especially weaving.

Young Socrates: Beautiful.

B **Stranger:** This is also in fact why we ventured the story, in order that it might be shown not only that, as regards herd-nurture, all compete for it with the man we're now seeking, but also in order that we might see more lucidly that very one whom alone it befits—because he has the care of human nurture, in accordance with the paradigm of shepherds and cowherds—to be deemed worthy of that form of address.

Young Socrates: Correct.

C **Stranger:** I at least, Socrates, think that this figure of the divine herdsman is still greater than the one that accords with the king, while the statesmen who are around nowadays are, in their natures, much more similar to those who are ruled and have partaken much more closely in their education and nurture.

Young Socrates: Altogether so, I suppose.

Stranger: And yet, whether they're disposed by nature to be in this way or in that, they would not have to be sought out either less or more for all that.

Young Socrates: Of course.

Stranger: Then let's go back again to this point, to the art we were saying was self-commanding and was applied to animals, but yet had the care of them not individu-
D ally but in common, and which at that time we readily called herd-nurture—you remember?

Young Socrates: Yes.

Stranger: And so, somewhere in there we were missing the mark, for nowhere did we take hold of or name the statesman, but through our assignment of names, he eluded us and escaped.

Young Socrates: How?

Stranger: All the other herdsmen, I suppose, share this trait, namely, the nurturing of their respective herds; but we attached the name to the statesman, though it doesn't

apply, when we ought to have attached some name
common to them all taken together.[19]   E

Young Socrates: What you say is true—if, in fact, there happened to be such a name.

Stranger: And how was it not the case that *tending* was, in
fact, somehow common to them all, since nurture had
in no way been specified, nor any other business? But
by naming it a certain herd-minding or tending or also
some other sort of care-giving art, which holds for all
herdsmen, it was possible to cover the statesman as
well, together with the others, since the account indicated that we ought to do so.

Young Socrates: Correct. But now in what manner would
the next division have been made?   276A

Stranger: In just the same way that we earlier divided herd-
nurture into footed and winged animals, and then into
unmixed and horn-shorn—with these same distinctions we could, I suppose, have continued to divide
herd-minding and have comprehended in the account
both kingship now and kingship under Cronos.

Young Socrates: It appears so; but now I'm looking for what
comes next.

Stranger: It's plain that if the name "herd-minding" had
been uttered, the contention of some that kingship is   B
in no way "care" would never have arisen for us, as
back then it was justly contended that there's no art
among us worthy of this title "nurturer," and if there
were one, this art would pertain to many others first
and more so than to any of the kings.

Young Socrates: Correct.

Stranger: But no other art would be willing to claim to be care
of the entire human community more than and prior to
kingship, and to be an art of rule over all humans.   C

---

19   The meaning of the word we have translated as "nurturing" (*trephein*)
is "feeding." The alternatives that the stranger is about to propose—
tending (*therapeuein*), minding (*komidzein*), and care-giving (*epimel-
ein*)—all have much broader meanings. See 276B-D and Glossary under "herd."

Young Socrates: Correctly put.

Stranger: And after this, Socrates, do we see that, right at the very end, a large error was again being made?

Young Socrates: Which error?

Stranger: This one, that even if we had understood very well that there was a certain art of nurturing the two-footed herd, for all that, we ought not to have addressed it straight off as the kingly and statesmanly art, as if it had been brought to completion.

Young Socrates: What else should we have done?

D   **Stranger:** In the first place, as we were just saying, we ought to have re-rigged the name, directing it toward care rather than nurture, and then cut this, for it might still admit of cuts that are not small.[20]

Young Socrates: Which ones?

Stranger: Insofar, I suppose, as we would have divided off the divine herdsman from the human caregiver.

Young Socrates: Correct.

Stranger: And again it was necessary to cut in two the assigned care-giving art.

Young Socrates: In what way?

Stranger: Into the forcible and the voluntary.

Young Socrates: Why's that?

E   **Stranger:** It's just here that we made an error earlier, I suppose, when, more naïvely than was needful, we put king and tyrant together in the same group, although both the men themselves and the manner of rule of each of them are very dissimilar.

Young Socrates: True.

Stranger: But should we now go back and correct ourselves and, just as I was saying, divide human care-giving in two, into the forcible and the voluntary?

---

20   The re-naming should have been done, and the additional divisions added, before the summing up at 267A-C.

Young Socrates: By all means.

Stranger: And addressing the care of those who are forced as, I suppose, tyrannical, and the voluntary herd-minding of voluntary two-footed animals as statesmanly, should we declare in turn that the man who has this art and care is king and statesman in his very being?

Young Socrates: Well, stranger, at least it seems as though   277A
our showing-forth of the statesman would in this way be complete.

Stranger: That would be a fine thing for us. However, not you alone but I in common with you must share that opinion about these matters. But now, in my opinion at least, the king doesn't yet appear to have his complete shape for us, but just as makers of human statues in their eagerness sometimes, in an untimely way, pile on accretions more numerous and larger than are needed and so slow down each of their works, we did   B
that as well just now: in order that we might make plain the error of our previous discourse with an eye to speed and in grand fashion, and deeming that it befitted the case of the king to invent great examples for ourselves and raise up a marvelous mass of myth, we were compelled to make use of a greater part of it than was needed. Therefore, we've made the showing-forth too long and for all that didn't give the story an ending. Instead, our account, just like an animal-painting,   C
seems, simply put, to have an adequate external outline but not yet to have received the sort of clarity that comes with pigments and blending of colors. And yet, for those capable of following, it's more fitting to make every animal plain in language and argument, rather than through painting and handicraft in general; but for the others, through handicrafts.

Young Socrates: That's correct, but make plain in what way you're saying we haven't yet spoken adequately.

D   **Stranger:** It's hard, my young genius, to indicate any of the greater matters adequately without using paradigms.[21] For it seems as though each of us, knowing everything as in a dream, is then ignorant again of everything when, as it were, awake—

Young Socrates: What are you saying?

Stranger: It's really absurd, but I do seem at this moment to have stirred up the condition we're in regarding knowledge.

Young Socrates: Why exactly?

Stranger: My very paradigm, blessed boy, is likewise also in need of a paradigm!

E   **Young Socrates:** What's that? Tell me and don't shrink back on my account.

Stranger: It must be told then, since you for your part are ready to follow. We know, I suppose, that children, when they're just becoming experienced with letters—

Young Socrates: What?

Stranger: —discern sufficiently each of the letters in the shortest and easiest of the syllables and become capable of pronouncing true things about those.

278A   **Young Socrates:** Of course.

Stranger: But then again, being doubtful about these very same letters in other syllables, they make mistakes in both opinion and speech.

Young Socrates: By all means.

Stranger: Now isn't the following the easiest and most beautiful way to bring these children to the letters that aren't yet recognized?

Young Socrates: What way?

---

21   Paradigm, in Greek, is *paradeigma*, from *para*, "alongside of," and *deiknynai*, "to show." A paradigm is something shown alongside something else (see Glossary). The word first occurs at 275B. Various words meaning "show" abound in this stretch of the dialogue (277A–278C).

Stranger: To lead them back, first to those cases in which they were correctly judging these same letters, and, while leading them back, to set alongside them the ones not yet recognized, and by throwing them side by side to indicate that there's the same similarity and nature in both intertwinings, until the letters that are truly judged have been shown as juxtaposed with all the ones about which there's ignorance, and having been shown, thereby becoming paradigms, bring it about that each one of all the letters in all the syllables is always addressed on the same terms with itself: as other when it's other than other letters, and same when it's the same.

B

C

Young Socrates: That's altogether so.

Stranger: Have we, then, adequately comprehended this— that the generation of a paradigm occurs at that time, when what is the same in something other that's sundered from it is correctly judged and, through comparison, brings to completion one true opinion about each of them as about both together?

Young Socrates: It appears so.

Stranger: Should we wonder, then, if our soul, which is by nature affected in this same way regarding the elements of all things,[22] is at one time made stable by the truth regarding each single element in certain groups, but then at another time is adrift regarding all the elements in others, and somehow or other correctly judges some mixtures of them, but goes back to being ignorant of these same elements when they're transposed into the long and not so easy syllables of practical life.

D

Young Socrates: No, indeed, it's nothing to be wondered at.

Stranger: For how else, my friend, might anyone who starts from false opinion attain to even some small part of the truth and acquire intelligence?

E

Young Socrates: Pretty much in no way at all.

---

22   The Greek word for element—*stoicheion*—is the same as the word for letter.

Stranger: So if that's how these things are naturally disposed, then would both you and I be at all out of tune if we first attempted to see the nature of paradigm in general in another, small paradigm that was particular, and—intending afterwards from somewhere or other to bring this same form, although it's derived from lesser things, to bear on the king's form, which is greatest—if we attempted, through a paradigm, to recognize by art the tendance of those things pertaining to a city, in order that wakefulness instead of sleep might arise for us?

Young Socrates: That's by all means correct.

279A **Stranger:** Once again the earlier argument must be taken up—that since thousands contend with the kingly kind for care concerning cities, we must separate off all these and leave only that man behind.[23] And to this end, we declared that we had need of some paradigm.

Young Socrates: Very much so.

Stranger: So then, what paradigm with the same business as statesmanship, but very small, could someone set alongside this and so discover adequately what's being sought? By Zeus, Socrates, if we don't have any other thing at hand, should we choose the art of *weaving*, and, if it seems best to you, not all of this art?[24] For the art concerned with things woven out of wool will doubtless suffice; once chosen, even this part of it would perhaps testify to what we want.

B

Young Socrates: Of course.

Stranger: So then, just as in the earlier arguments we divided each thing by cutting parts from parts, why don't we do this same thing now concerning weaving, and by going through everything quickly in as few words as possible come back again to what's useful at present?

C

Young Socrates: How do you mean?

Stranger: I'll make the way itself my answer to you.

---

23   See 267E-268D. See also 275B and 276B.

24   For a description of the art of weaving, see Appendix A.

Young Socrates: Most beautifully put.

Stranger: Well then, all the things we have that we craft and acquire are in some cases for the sake of doing something, in others defenses against suffering; and of defenses some are protective potions both divine and human, others barriers; and of barriers some are D armaments for war, others screens; and of screens some are curtains, others protections against winter storms and summer-sun; and of protections some are shelters, others coverings, and of coverings some are rugs spread beneath and others wrap-arounds; and of wrap-arounds some are of one piece and others composites; and of composites some are stitched, others E bound together without stitches; and of the unstitched ones some are made of plant fibers from the earth, others made of hair; and of the ones made from hair some are glued together by liquids and clay, others themselves bound together with themselves. To these very defenses and coverings, worked by fastening them together with themselves, we give the name "cloaks." And as for the art that takes care of cloaks in particular—just as before we spoke of the art that takes care of 280A the city as political,[25] so now too, shouldn't we address this one, naming it after its own business, as cloak-working? And further, should we say that the art of weaving, insofar as its major portion is involved in the workings of cloaks, differs in nothing but name from this cloak-working, just as back then kingship differed from statesmanship?

Young Socrates: Most correct.

Stranger: So after this, let's reflect that someone might perhaps think that the art of weaving cloaks, thus described, has been described adequately, since he was not able to B comprehend that it was not yet marked off from the arts whose work is closely related to it, although it had been set apart from many other kindred ones.

Young Socrates: Which kindred ones? Tell me.

---

25   The stranger stresses the connection between *polis*, city, and *politikê*, here translated "political." See Glossary under "city."

Stranger: You didn't follow what was said, as it appears. So it seems one must go back again, beginning from the end. For just now we cut off from it its kindred art, if you comprehend the family relation, separating the composition of spreads according to "throwing-round" and "throwing-under"—

Young Socrates: I understand.

C   **Stranger:** —and in fact we also divided off all the crafts-manship that works with flax and broom-cords and all those plant fibers that we just now spoke of as analogous to sinews; and then we marked off the art of felting and the composition that uses piercing and stitching, most of which is the shoemaking art.

Young Socrates: By all means.

Stranger: And so then the treatment of one-piece leather-worked coverings, and the arts of shelters, all those that engage in house-building and carpentry in general and are sheltering arts involved in all the other arts of water-

D   proofing—these we removed altogether, and as many screening arts as provide preventive works against thefts and deeds of violence, being concerned with both the generation of lid-making-works and the joining of doors-and-frames, which were assigned as portions of the art of fastening. And we cut off the armor-making art, which is a section of the great and various barrier-making power. And we also marked off right away, at

E   the beginning, the magic art that's concerned with protective potions, the whole of it, and we had left, as it would seem, that very art we were seeking—the one that defends from winter storms, fashions barriers of wool, and is called by the name of the weaving art.

Young Socrates: That seems to be the case.

Stranger: But, my boy, this isn't yet completely stated. For he who, in the beginning, takes in hand the fashioning

281A   of cloaks appears to do the opposite of weaving.

Young Socrates: How?

Stranger: The business of weaving is, I suppose, some sort of intertwining—

Young Socrates: Yes.

Stranger: —but another is the art of taking apart things that have been composed and felted together.

Young Socrates: What's that?

Stranger: The work of the art of one who cards. Or shall we dare to call carding weaving, and refer to the carder as being a weaver?

Young Socrates: No way.

Stranger: And surely if someone goes on to address the art of fashioning the warp and the woof as weaving, he utters a name both incredible and false.   B

Young Socrates: Of course.

Stranger: What about this? Shall we set down the entire art of brushing and of mending as in no way whatsoever a sort of care and tending of clothes, or say that all these too, in their entirety, are arts of weaving?

Young Socrates: No way.

Stranger: But surely all these together will in fact contend with the power of weaving over the tending and generating of cloaks, yielding to it the greatest part, though assigning to themselves great parts as well.

Young Socrates: Entirely so.   C

Stranger: Now furthermore, in addition to these, we must believe that the arts that are crafters of the instruments by which the works of weaving are accomplished will in fact claim to be joint-causes in every woven thing.

Young Socrates: Most correct.

Stranger: Then will our account of the weaving art—the part of it we selected—have been adequately determined if we set down that, of all the arts that care for woolen clothing, it's the most beautiful and greatest; or would   D we be saying something true, yet neither clear nor at all perfect, until we stripped away from it all those other arts?

Young Socrates: Correct.

Stranger: Then after this, mustn't we do what we're saying, in order that our account may proceed step-by-step?

Young Socrates: Of course.

Stranger: First, then, let's observe that there are two arts involved in all things that are brought to a finish—

Young Socrates: Which ones?

Stranger: —one being the joint-cause of the generating, the other the cause itself.

Young Socrates: How's that?

E   **Stranger:** All those arts that do not craft the thing itself, although they provide tools for the crafting arts, in the absence of which the work assigned to each of the arts wouldn't ever have been accomplished—these are *joint-causes*, while those that produce the thing itself are *causes*.[26]

Young Socrates: That makes sense, at any rate.

Stranger: Next, then, shall we claim that the arts having to do with both spindles and combs, and all the other tools that share in generating the things we wear, are all *joint-causes*, while those that tend and craft those things are *causes*?

Young Socrates: Most correct.

282A   **Stranger:** Now among causes are the arts of washing and mending and all the tending concerning these things; and since the art of refurbishing is large, it seems especially reasonable to comprehend the entire portion of it here by naming it the fulling art.

Young Socrates: Beautiful.

Stranger: And surely carding and spinning and all the parts in turn concerned with the making itself of the clothing we're talking about, are some one art among those everyone has a name for—wool-working.

B   **Young Socrates:** Of course.

---

26   This distinction comes up at *Phaedo* 99A-B and *Timaeus* 46C-E.

Stranger: Now there are two paired sections of the wool-working art, and each one of these two is at the same time by nature part of a pair of arts.

Young Socrates: How's that?

Stranger: The work of carding and half the combing art and all the processes that set apart from one another things that are put together, all this, to affirm it as one, belongs, I suppose, to wool-working itself—and there was, in our view, a certain pair of great arts ranging over all, the arts of combination and separation—

Young Socrates: Yes.

Stranger: Well then, to the art of separating belongs both the carding art and all the things mentioned just now; for the art of separating both in wool and in warp-threads, brought about in one way with comb and in another with hands, has all the names mentioned just now.

C

Young Socrates: By all means.

Stranger: Now again, let's take up something that arises within combination that's at once a portion of it and of wool-working; and let's leave aside here all that belonged to the separating art and cut wool-working in two, into a separating and a combining section.

Young Socrates: Let it have been divided.

Stranger: Well then, Socrates, the portion that belongs at once to the combining art and to the wool-working art must in turn be divided by you if in fact we mean to take hold adequately of the weaving art that was mentioned earlier.

D

Young Socrates: Then it should be divided.

Stranger: It certainly should be. And, in fact, let's say that one part of it is twisting, the other intertwining.

Young Socrates: Am I understanding? For you seem to me to be calling the part concerned with the working up of the warp twisting.

Stranger: Not only that, but also that of the woof. Or will we find any generating of it that doesn't involve twisting?

Young Socrates: No way.

Stranger: So mark off each of these, too—the marking off could perhaps turn out to be timely for you.

E

Young Socrates: Where?

Stranger: Here. Among the products that concern carding, do we say that something that's both lengthened and has breadth is a "stretch"?

Young Socrates: Yes.

Stranger: Now the part of this that's twisted by the spindle and becomes solid thread—declare it to be the warp thread and the art that directs it "warp-thread making."

Young Socrates: Correct.

Stranger: And all the stretches in turn that receive a loose twisting together, while with respect to the pull of the comb they have a degree of softness suited to their entwining within the warp—these, then, once spun, let's declare to be the woof, and the art that's assigned to them "woof-thread making."

283A

Young Socrates: Most correct.

Stranger: And surely the part of the weaving art that we were proposing is by now plain, I suppose, to everyone. For regarding the portion of the art of combination engaged in wool working—whenever it produces a twining by neat intertwining of woof and warp, we address the entire thing twined as a woolen garment and the art directed at it as weaving.

Young Socrates: Most correct.

Stranger: Alright. Then why in the world didn't we answer right away that weaving was the twining of woof and warp, but went around in a circle, vainly marking off a great many parts?

B

Young Socrates: Not to me, stranger—nothing of what was said seemed to have been uttered in vain.

Stranger: And that's nothing to be wondered at; but perhaps, blessed boy, it might seem so. Then with respect to such a sickness, should it come upon you often later on—which would be nothing to wonder at—listen to a certain account that's fittingly uttered about all such matters.   C

Young Socrates: Just tell it.

Stranger: First, then, let's look at all excess and deficiency, in order that in each case we may, in such engagements, proportionately praise or blame the things said when they are needlessly long-winded or the opposite.

Young Socrates: So we should.

Stranger: If our account proved to be about these very things, it would, I think, prove to be correct.

Young Socrates: About what things?

Stranger: About length and brevity and about all super-abundance and deficiency. For surely the art of mea-   D
surement is concerned with all these.

Young Socrates: Yes.

Stranger: Then let's divide it into two parts; for they're needed for what we're now striving after.

Young Socrates: Please say where the division is made.

Stranger: Here. One part has to do with the reciprocal com-muning in greatness and smallness, the other with the being that's necessary to generation.

Young Socrates: How do you mean?

Stranger: Doesn't it seem to you that one must say that, ac-cording to nature, the greater is greater than nothing other than the lesser, and again the lesser less than the   E
greater, and than nothing else?

Young Socrates: To me at least it seems so.

Stranger: What about this? Won't we also say that there genuinely comes to be that which exceeds the nature of due measure or is exceeded by this nature, whether in words or also in deeds, and that in this respect in particular bad and good men differ among us?

Young Socrates: So it appears.

Stranger: Then one must set down this twofold being and distinguishing of the great and the small; but we must not say, as we did a moment ago, that they must be only in relation to each other, but rather, as was stated just now, one way of being must be spoken of as "in relation to one another," the other in turn as "in relation to due measure."[27] Would we like to learn the point of this?

Young Socrates: Certainly.

284A **Stranger:** If one will allow the nature of the greater to be in relation to nothing other than in relation to the less, it won't ever be in relation to due measure, isn't that so?

Young Socrates: Yes, that's so.

Stranger: Then, by this account, won't we destroy both the arts themselves and all their works, and won't we in particular obliterate what is now being sought, statesmanship, and what was just described, the weaving art? For all such arts surely keep strict guard in their actions over the more and less of due measure, not on the view that due measure *is not* but that it is difficult. B And it's exactly in this manner, by preserving measure, that they produce all good and beautiful things.

Young Socrates: Certainly.

Stranger: Then if we obliterated the statesman's art, won't our subsequent search for the kingly science be at an impasse?

Young Socrates: Very much so.

Stranger: Well then, just as in the case of the sophist we compelled non-being to *be*, since it was down this way that the argument escaped us,[28] so now too, mustn't the more and the less in turn be compelled to be measured, not in relation to each other alone but also in C relation to the generating of due measure? Indeed, it's

---

27   On the two kinds of measure, see Aristotle's *Nicomachean Ethics* II, 1106a27-1107a2 and VI, 1138b18-25.

28   See *Sophist* 241D. For the language of descent within a set of divisions, see 235B-C and 236D.

not possible for either a statesman or anyone else to have become, indisputably, knowledgeable about matters of action if this isn't jointly agreed on.

Young Socrates: Then now too, we should most certainly do the same thing.

Stranger: This, Socrates, is still more of a task than that other one; and yet we surely remember how great its length was! But it's certainly just to hypothesize about them some such thing as this.

Young Socrates: What sort of thing?

Stranger: That at some point we shall need what was just said for the showing-forth of the precise itself. But that the present demonstration is beautiful and sufficient the following account seems to me to support magnificently: We must alike hold that all the arts *are*, and that greater and less are measured not only in relation to each other but also in relation to the generating of due measure. For if this *is*, then they *are*, and if those arts *are*, then this *is* as well; but if either of these *is not*, then neither of them ever *will be*. D

Young Socrates: That's correct, but now what comes next? E

Stranger: It's plain that we should divide the art of measurement in accordance with what's been said, cutting it in two in this way: by setting down as one portion of it all arts that measure number and length and depth and breadth and swiftness in relation to their opposites, while setting down as another those that measure in relation to due measure, the fitting, the timely, the needful, and however many of all such things as have left their abode in the extremes and migrated toward the middle.

Young Socrates: Yes, each section you spoke of is really big, and the two differ hugely from each other.

Stranger: For what many of the clever sometimes say, Socrates, thinking they're in fact uttering something wise—that the art of measurement is, after all, about all the things that come into being—this very thing 285A turns out to be what was just said.[29] For in some manner everything that's artful has participated in measurement; but since people aren't accustomed to look into things by dividing them according to forms, they right away throw these things that are so different together in the same group, deeming them similar, and then they do the opposite of this with other things, failing to divide them according to parts; though it's

B   needful, whenever someone at first perceives the community of many things, not to desist before he sees the differences within it, all those that lie within forms, and then again, in the case of all sorts of dissimilarities, whenever they're seen in multitudes, to be incapable of becoming crestfallen and stopping before he encompasses and encloses with the being of some kind all the things that belong within the confines of one similarity. Now then, enough has been said about these things and about deficiencies and excesses; but let's just keep in mind that two kinds of the measuring art have been

C   discovered concerning them, and let's remember what we claim they are.

Young Socrates: We'll remember.

Stranger: So after this argument let's admit another that concerns both the very things we're searching for and every engagement in such arguments.

Young Socrates: Which one?

Stranger: If someone should ask us about the gathering of students learning about letters, where one of them is asked what letters make up any word, should we declare to him in this case that the search arises more for

D   the sake of the one word that's been proposed or for becoming more literate about all proposed words?

Young Socrates: It's plain that it's for becoming more literate about all of them.

Stranger: And now, what in turn about our search concerning the statesman? Has it been proposed for the sake

---

29   An allusion to Protagoras' famous dictum—treated at length in the *Theaetetus*—that "man is the measure of all things."

of this man himself more than for our becoming more dialectical about all things?

Young Socrates: This too is plain: that it's for becoming more dialectical about all things.[30]

Stranger: Surely no one in his right mind would be willing to hunt down the account of weaving for the sake of weaving itself. But it has eluded most men, I think, that in the case of some of the things that *are*, certain perceptible similarities are by nature easy to understand,   E
and these are not difficult to make plain—they give no trouble and need no argument—whenever anyone wishes to indicate them easily to someone who asks for an account about one of them. But then again, for the things that *are* and are greatest and most honorable, there's no image that's been worked out perspicu-   286A
ously for human beings such that, when it was shown, he who wanted to fill up the soul of the inquirer by adapting the image to one of his senses will fill the soul sufficiently. Therefore we must practice being able to receive and give a verbal account of each thing. For bodiless things, since they're most beautiful and greatest, are shown clearly only in an account and in nothing else, and it's for the sake of these that all that is now being said is being said. But in every case, practice in lesser things is easier than in greater ones.   B

Young Socrates: Most beautifully put.

Stranger: Now then, let us remember that for the sake of which we said all this about these matters.

Young Socrates: Which things?

Stranger: It wasn't least because of that very irritation with the long-winded speech we tolerated irritatedly regarding the weaving art, and regarding the unwinding of the all, and, in the case of the sophist, regarding

---

30   The stranger describes "dialectical knowledge" at *Sophist* 253B-E. For Socrates' account of dialectic, see *Republic* VI, 511B, and VII, 531D-534E. See Glossary under "dialectical."

C

the being of non-being.[31] We observed that they had too great a length, and we reproached ourselves in all these cases, fearing that we'd be saying things irrelevant as well as long. In order, then, that we might in no way experience this sort of thing again, declare that what went before was said by the pair of us because of all this.

Young Socrates: Let it be so. Only say what comes next.

Stranger: I say, then, that, remembering what was said just now, you and I should bestow in each instance praise and blame for the brevity as well as the length of whatever we were at that time speaking about, not by judging the lengths in relation to each other, but—according to the part of the measuring art that we then declared

D

must be remembered—in relation to the fitting.

Young Socrates: Correct.

Stranger: Not all things, however, in relation to this. For we won't have any additional need for a length adapted with a view to pleasure, except as some by-product. And in turn, in relation to the search for what's been set before us—how we may discover it as easily and quickly as possible—the account urges us to cherish that as second but not as first, but far rather and first to honor the pursuit itself of being able to divide by forms

E

and, moreover, to take seriously an account, even if it be told at great length, when it makes the listener more capable of discovery, and to be in no way vexed by its length—and to do the same if in turn the account is very short. And yet again besides this, he who blames the extent of speeches in such discussions and doesn't tolerate their going around in a circle—such a person, the account urges, we should not let go so very quickly

287A

or directly just because he blamed them for being long-spoken. But he must also show in addition that one must assume that if these things had been briefer, they would've made those engaged with them more dialec-

---

31   See 277C and 283B. Although the stranger in the *Sophist* never complains explicitly about the length of his account of non-being, he does worry openly at the outset of the dialogue about the length of the arguments that lie ahead (217A).

tical and more capable of discovering the way of making beings plain in an account; but one should think nothing of the blame and praise from other people in relation to other standards in these sorts of accounts, nor even seem to hear them at all. But enough of these things, if you too share this opinion; so let's go back again to the statesman and bring to bear on him the paradigm of weaving that we talked about earlier.   B

Young Socrates: Beautifully put, and let's do what you say.

Stranger: The king, then, has been thoroughly separated off, at least from the many arts that share his field, or rather from all those having to do with herds. But there remain throughout a city itself, we declare, the arts of both the joint-causes and the causes—which are the first arts that must be divided off from each other.

Young Socrates: Correct.

Stranger: Well, do you know that it's difficult to cut them in two? But the cause, as I think, will be no less manifest   C to us as we proceed.

Young Socrates: Then that's what we should do.

Stranger: Well then, let's divide them limb by limb, like a sacrificial animal, since we don't have the power to do it by two. For one must always cut as far as possible with an eye to the number nearest.

Young Socrates: How, then, should we do it in the present case?

Stranger: Just as we were saying earlier. However many arts were providing tools for the weaving art—all these, I suppose, we set down at that time as joint-causes.

Young Socrates: Yes.

Stranger: So now too, we must do this very same thing, and to a still greater degree than we did then. For all   D these arts that craft some tool, small or great, throughout a city, must be set down as being joint-causes. For without these, neither the city nor the statesman's art would ever arise—but then again, I suppose, we won't set down their work as that of the kingly art.

Young Socrates: No, we won't.

Stranger: And yet, we're attempting a thing difficult to accomplish when we go about separating off this kind from the others; for the person who says that anything at all among the things that *are* is, as it were, a tool of at least some one thing, seems to have said something persuasive. In any case, let's speak of this in turn as another among the possessions in a city.

E

Young Socrates: What sort of thing is it?

Stranger: Let's say that it's not something having this power. For it's compacted not for the purpose of being a cause of generation, like a tool, but for the safe-keeping of the thing that's been crafted.

Young Socrates: What sort of thing is it?

Stranger: It's this, that manifold form which, having been worked up for dry goods or liquids, for things that go on the fire or not on the fire, we call, by a single designation, "container"—an especially widespread form that's simply not at all suited, as I think, to the science that's being sought.

288A

Young Socrates: Of course.

Stranger: Now a third form of possessions other than these and altogether large must be taken into view—land-based and water-based, much-wandering and unwandering, honorable and dishonorable, yet having one name, because all are for the sake of some seating, always turning up as a chair for someone.

Young Socrates: What sort of thing is it?

Stranger: We call it, I suppose, a "bearer"—not at all a work that belongs to the statesman's art, but much rather to carpentry and ceramics and bronze-shaping.

Young Socrates: I understand.

B

Stranger: What about a fourth? Mustn't we speak of a form that's other than these, one within which are the greater part of the things mentioned earlier, all clothing and most arms, and all encompassing walls of earth and stone, and a thousand other things? But since all of these have been worked up for the sake of defending, they would very justly be addressed as a whole as a defense, and this—most of it—would be thought more correctly to be a work that belongs to the house-building art and weaving, much more than to the statesman's art.

Young Socrates: By all means.

Stranger: Would we be willing to set down as a fifth what   C
concerns decoration and the art of painting, and all the things that use this and music to bring imitations to completion, produced only for our pleasure, and would it be justly embraced by one name?

Young Socrates: What name?

Stranger: Something, I suppose, is called a plaything?

Young Socrates: Certainly.

Stranger: Well then, it will be fitting that this one name be used to address all these, for not one of them is for the sake of seriousness, but all are accomplished for the sake of play.

Young Socrates: This too I still pretty much understand.   D

Stranger: What provides, for all these things, bodies out of which and in which all of the arts now mentioned do their crafting—a manifold form that's the offspring of many other arts—won't we set it down as a sixth?

Young Socrates: What exactly do you mean?

Stranger: Both gold and silver and all the things that get mined, and all the things that tree-cutting and slicing in general provide, by cutting, to carpentry and to the twining art; and furthermore, both the art that strips bark from plants and the leather-cutting art that   E
removes skins from ensouled bodies, and all the arts concerned with such things, and those that work up corks and papyrus and cords and provide, for crafting, composite forms out of kinds that are not composed. We address it all as one thing, the first-born and in-composite possession for human beings, and one that's in no way the work of kingly science.

Young Socrates: Beautiful.

Stranger: The acquisition of nurture, then, and whatever things relevant to the body, which mix parts of themselves in with parts of the body, have been allotted a certain power to tend it, must be said to be seventh. We name the whole thing as being our nourishment, unless we have some other, more beautiful label to put on it; and in putting everything down to the art of farming as well as the arts of hunting and exercising and healing and cooking, we will render it more correctly than if we gave it over to the statesman's art.

289A

Young Socrates: Of course.

Stranger: Whatever belongs to acquiring, then, has been pretty nearly mentioned within these seven kinds, I think, except the tame animals. But observe: It would have been most just for the first-born form to be put at the beginning, and after that, tool, container, bearer, defense, plaything, nourishment. But what we've left out, unless something large has eluded us, it's possible to fit into some one of these, such as the look of a coin and seals and every sort of stamp. For these have among themselves no large kind with a common field, but though they're dragged in by force—some into "ornament," others into "tools"—nevertheless they will at least be consonant. But as for the things that concern the acquisition of tame animals except slaves, herd-nurturing—which was previously divided into parts—comes to light as having embraced them all.

B

C

Young Socrates: By all means.

Stranger: And surely the remaining kind is that of slaves and all servants; and it's somewhere among them, I'm divining, that those contending with the king for the web itself will become manifest, just as previously those engaged in spinning and carding and all the other things we spoke of contended with weavers. But all the others, described as joint-causes, along with the works mentioned just now, have been removed and separated from a practice that's both kingly and statesmanly.

D

Young Socrates: That seems likely, at least.

Stranger: Come then, let's approach the remaining people and look at them from close up, so that we may know them more firmly.

Young Socrates: We should indeed.

Stranger: Now as for the greatest servants, when seen from this point of view, we find that they have a practice and condition that's the opposite of what we suspected.

Young Socrates: Who are they?

Stranger: Those bought and in this manner acquired, whom we can indisputably call slaves, and who are the last to pretend to any of the kingly art.   E

Young Socrates: Of course.

Stranger: What about this? Those among the free who willingly place themselves in service to the ones we've just mentioned—those who convey to one another, and distribute about, the products of farming and those of the other arts, some over market places, others ranging from city to city over the sea or on foot, exchanging currency both for other things and for itself—those to whom we have given the name silver-changers and traders and shipmasters and peddlers—do they contend for any of the statesman's art?   290A

Young Socrates: Perhaps, I suppose, for that aspect of it that deals with matters of trade.

Stranger: But surely we won't ever find those readily serving all men as wage-earners and laborers making a claim to kingship.

Young Socrates: Of course not.

Stranger: But then what about those who on each occasion minister to us in the following things?

Young Socrates: What sorts of things do you mean, and which people?

Stranger: The heralding tribe is among them, and all those who by frequent service become adept in letters, and some others who are awfully clever at accomplishing   B many other jobs concerning public office. What, then, shall we call these?

Young Socrates: Just what you did now, servants, but don't call them rulers in the cities.

Stranger: But surely, as I at least think, I wasn't seeing a dream when I said that somewhere in this place those who especially contend for the statesman's art will appear. And yet to search for these people in some sub-

C servient station would seem to be utterly absurd.

Young Socrates: Absolutely.

Stranger: Then let's engage still more closely with those who haven't yet been tested. They are the ones who deal in divination and have a portion of a certain ministerial science; for I suppose they're considered interpreters from gods to human beings.

Young Socrates: Yes.

Stranger: And surely the priest-kind in turn, as what is lawful dictates, is knowledgeable in how, through sacrifices, to offer gifts from us to gods according to what's agreeable to them, while also, by prayers, to ask for the acquisi-

D tion of good things that come from them to us; and both these, I suppose, are portions of a ministerial art.

Young Socrates: At least it appears so.

Stranger: Finally, then, we seem to me to be close to fixing on some sort of track that leads to where we're going. For indeed the figure of the priests and that of the diviners are very much filled up with pride, and gain an august reputation because of the greatness of their undertakings, so that in Egypt it's not allowed for a king

E to rule apart from the priestly art; but if he happens to have forced his way in out of some other kind beforehand, then it's necessary for him to be initiated afterwards into the priestly kind. And moreover, in many places among the Greeks too, one would discover that the greatest of the sacrifices dealing with such things are assigned, for their performance, to the greatest public offices. And especially among you who live in this place, what I mean is not least of all plain, for they

claim that here the most august and most ancestral of the ancient sacrifices are given to the one who gets to be king by lot.

Young Socrates: Yes, entirely so.

Stranger: Well then, we must look into these people who are kings by lot and also priests,[32] along with their servants, and a certain other very large mob that has just recently become very plain to us now that the earlier groups have been separated off.   291A

Young Socrates: And just whom do you mean?

Stranger: Some very strange people.

Young Socrates: In what way, exactly?

Stranger: Theirs is a kind made up of every which tribe, at least it appears so looking at them just now. Many of the men are like lions and centaurs and other such creatures, and a great many like satyrs and weak beasts of many wiles; and they quickly exchange both their looks and power with one another. And yet, just now, Socrates, I think I've caught sight of the men.   B

Young Socrates: Please speak, for you seem to be glimpsing something strange.

Stranger: Yes, for it's through ignorance that the strange befalls everyone. That's exactly what I too experienced even now. I was suddenly confused when I saw the chorus concerned with the affairs of cities.   C

Young Socrates: Which one?

Stranger: The one that of all the sophists is the greatest wizard and the one most experienced in this art. Although awfully difficult to divide off, divided off he must be from the ones who are statesmanly and kingly in their very being, if we are to see clearly what's being sought.

Young Socrates: But surely we mustn't let this go.

---

32   In Athens, there was a group of nine officials called *archontes*, rulers, all chosen by lot. The one charged with mounting religious events and trying religious cases was termed *basileus*, king. See Aristotle's *Constitution of Athens* 3, 22, 57.

Stranger: Not in my opinion at least. And tell me this.

Young Socrates: What?

D **Stranger:** Isn't monarchy, in our view, one of the types of political rule?[33]

Young Socrates: Yes.

Stranger: And after monarchy someone might, I suppose, speak of the holding of power by the few.

Young Socrates: Of course.

Stranger: And isn't a third figure of regime the rule of the multitude, called democracy by name?

Young Socrates: Entirely so.

Stranger: And don't these, which are three, become five in a certain manner, because two of them bring forth out of themselves other names in addition to themselves?

Young Socrates: Which ones exactly?

E **Stranger:** Nowadays, I suppose, people look to the forcible and the voluntary, and poverty and wealth, and law and lawlessness, as they arise within regimes, dividing each of the two in two, and address monarchy—on the grounds that it's been furnished with two forms—with two names, the one tyranny, the other kingship.

Young Socrates: Certainly.

Stranger: And the city that's mastered by a few they address in each case as aristocracy and oligarchy.

Young Socrates: Entirely so.

292A **Stranger:** In the case of democracy, however, whether the multitude rules over those with property forcibly or voluntarily, and whether it guards the laws precisely or not, no one is ever in the habit of changing its name.

---

33   Classic treatments of the number and basic character of the different political regimes may be found in *Republic* VIII and IX, and in Aristotle's *Politics* III (especially 1279a 24-1280a7) and *Ethics* VIII, 1169a31-b24.

Young Socrates: True.

Stranger: Then what about this? Do we believe that any of these regimes is the correct one when it's marked off by these distinguishing marks—by one and few and many, and by wealth and poverty, and by the forcible and voluntary, and whether the regime happens to come about with writings or without laws?

Young Socrates: Well, what prevents it?

Stranger: Just take a clearer look by following in this direction.   B

Young Socrates: Which?

Stranger: Shall we stand by, or disagree with, what was said in the beginning?

Young Socrates: To which thing exactly are you referring?

Stranger: We affirmed, I believe, that kingly rule was one of the sciences.

Young Socrates: Yes.

Stranger: And not just one of all these, but we singled it out from the others as doubtless being a certain judging and supervising science.[34]

Young Socrates: Yes.

Stranger: And from the supervising science we singled out one for soulless works, another for animals. And parti-   C
tioning in this very manner we have gone ever forward to this point, not forgetting that it is a science but not yet being able to be fully precise about the "what sort."

Young Socrates: Correctly put.

Stranger: Do we, then, understand this very thing—that the distinguishing mark concerning these regimes should not be few or many, not the voluntary or the involun-tary, not poverty or riches, but a certain science, if in fact we're to follow what went before?

Young Socrates: But it's impossible not to do that.   D

Stranger: Then, of necessity, we must now look into this

---

34   For these divisions, see 258B, 260B-C, and 261B-C.

matter in the following way: In which of these, if any, does science concerning the rule of human beings, the one that is just about the hardest and greatest to acquire happen to come about? For we must catch sight of it, so that we may behold which men are to be separated from the intelligent king—those who pretend to be, and persuade many that they are, statesmen, but in no way are.

Young Socrates: We must indeed do this very thing, as the argument told us to earlier.

E   **Stranger:** Then surely a multitude in a city doesn't seem able to acquire this science, does it?

Young Socrates: How could it?

Stranger: But in a city of a thousand men, is it possible that some hundred or even fifty could acquire it sufficiently?

Young Socrates: In that case, it would be the easiest of all the arts to acquire. For we know that in a city of a thousand men there would never come to be that many topnotch draught-players, not to mention kings, compared with those found among the other Greeks. For surely he who does have the kingly science, whether he rule or 293A   not, must, according to the foregoing argument, nevertheless be addressed as kingly.

Stranger: You recalled it beautifully. And what follows from this, I think, is that one must search for correct rule, whenever it proves correct, in the case of some one or two or altogether few.

Young Socrates: Certainly.

Stranger: While these men in fact, whether they rule the willing or the unwilling, whether according to writings or without writings, and whether they have wealth or are poor—one must consider them, just as we now hold, as B   exercising rule of whatever sort according to art. And not least of all do we consider doctors to be doctors, whether they heal us when we're willing or unwilling by cutting or burning or applying some other pain. And whether they do it according to writings or apart from writings, and whether they're poor or rich, we call them doctors not one bit less, just so long as they supervise by means of art, and, whether they purge or reduce us in some other way, or even increase us, provided that those who severally administer the treatment do so only for the good of our bodies, by making them better from worse, and so preserve the things C treated. In this way and in no other, as I think, we shall set this down as the only correct distinguishing mark of the doctor's rule, or of any other rule whatsoever.

Young Socrates: Absolutely.

Stranger: It's necessary, then, that among regimes too, as it seems, this is the superlatively correct one and the only regime in which one might discover rulers who are truly and not just seemingly knowledgeable, whether they rule according to laws or without laws, and whether they rule the willing or the unwilling, and whether they are poor or have wealth—one must D count none of these things at all as being in accord with any correctness whatsoever.

Young Socrates: Beautiful.

Stranger: And whether in fact by killing or also banishing some they purge the city for its good, or make it smaller by sending out colonies somewhere, like swarms of bees, or increase it by bringing in some other citizens from somewhere on the outside, so long as they make it better from worse and preserve it as far as they're able by using science and the just—this must be declared by us, at that time and according to such distin- E guishing marks, to be the only correct regime. And all the other regimes we speak of must be spoken of not as trueborn or as genuinely being, but as having imitated this one—those we speak of as having good laws with more beautiful results, the rest with uglier ones.

Young Socrates: Everything else, stranger, seems to have been said in a measured way; but that there must be ruling even without laws is a saying that's harder to hear.

Stranger: You got in a little ahead of me with your question, Socrates. For I was about to ask you whether you 294A accept all these things, or in fact find some one of the things said hard to take. But now it's become apparent that we'll want to go through this point about the correctness of rulers without laws.

Young Socrates: Of course.

Stranger: Now certainly in some manner it's plain that the art of law-giving belongs to the kingly art. Yet the best thing is not that the laws hold sway, but that a man does—the kingly man with intelligence.[35] Do you know in what way?

Young Socrates: What way do you mean exactly?

Stranger: In that law could never, by having comprehended
B   precisely what's most excellent and most just for all at the same time, command what's best. For the dissimilarities of both human beings and actions, and the never being at rest, so to speak, of any single thing among human things—these do not allow any art whatsoever to proclaim anything simply in any area concerning all things and for all time. We do grant these things, I suppose?

Young Socrates: Certainly.

Stranger: But we see the law pretty much straining in this very direction, just like some human being who's stubborn and ignorant and allows no one to do anything
C   against his own order nor to ask any questions, not even if something new contrary to the command he himself uttered should turn out to be better for someone.

Young Socrates: True. For the law acts ineptly toward each of us, as you've said just now.

Stranger: Then isn't it impossible for what proves to be simple throughout all times to stay in good condition with respect to what's never simple?

Young Socrates: It looks that way.

Stranger: For what reason, then, is it ever necessary to lay down laws, since in fact the law is not entirely correct?
D   The cause of this must be discovered.

---

35   Aristotle discusses the question of the rule of law versus that of an exceptional individual in the *Politics* (III.13.1283a23 ff.).

Young Socrates: Certainly.

Stranger: Then among you too, are there, as in other cities, something like practice sessions for people in groups, in running or in something else, for the sake of competing?

Young Socrates: In fact, a great many.

Stranger: Come now. Let's recall in memory the commands of those who in such offices train others by art.

Young Socrates: With respect to what?

Stranger: In that they don't believe there's room to do one-on-one detailed work, prescribing what's appropriate for each body, but instead think they must fashion more crudely an order for the advantage of bodies that holds for the most part and for most people.

E

Young Socrates: Beautiful.

Stranger: That's exactly why nowadays they also assign groups equal workouts, and start a run and a wrestle and all bodily workouts at the same time, and also stop them at the same time.

Young Socrates: That's so.

Stranger: Let us believe, then, that the lawgiver too, the one who is to supervise the herds with respect to the just and their contracts with each other, won't ever, by prescribing to all in a group, be up to delivering precisely what's appropriate to each.

295A

Young Socrates: That's likely, at any rate.

Stranger: But he will, I think, set down the law as something appropriate for most people and for the most part, and thus somehow crudely for each one of them, whether he delivers it in writings or in unwritten ways by setting down the law through ancestral customs.

Young Socrates: Correct.

Stranger: Correct, indeed. For how, Socrates, would anyone ever be up to prescribing what's appropriate with precision, always sitting by each person's side throughout life? Since if he were so able, being someone among

B

those who had genuinely taken hold of the kingly science, he would, as I think, scarcely ever put obstacles before himself by writing down these so-called laws.

Young Socrates: Not at least on the basis of what was just said, stranger.

Stranger: And even more, best of boys, on the basis of the things about to be pronounced.

Young Socrates: What things exactly?

Stranger: These. For let's say, just among ourselves, that a
C   doctor or even some trainer was about to leave home and was to be absent from those under his care for a long time, as he thinks—if he had thought that the trainees or the sick wouldn't remember what was prescribed, would he wish to write reminders for them, or what?

Young Socrates: Just that.

Stranger: But what if he came back, after being away from home for less time than he thought? Wouldn't he venture to substitute other things in place of those writings, if they happened to be better for the sick, because
D   winds or even something else occurred against expectation, one of those things from Zeus that are different from the usual? Would he persist in believing that he must not transgress the laws once anciently set down, nor himself prescribe others, nor must the sick man dare to do things different from what had been written, on the grounds that these were healing and healthful, and what happens differently was sick-making as well as not artful? Or wouldn't everything of that sort, at least if it turned up in science and true art, give rise
E   in all cases in every way to the greatest laughter about such law-givings?

Young Socrates: That's altogether so.

Stranger: But for him who has written, or has set down unwritten laws, about matters of just and unjust and beautiful and ugly and good and bad, for as many herds of humans as are severally pastured city by city according to the laws of those who wrote them—if he who wrote them with art arrived, or someone else like him, should he not indeed be allowed to prescribe other things contrary to these? Or wouldn't such a prohibition too appear in truth laughable, no less than the former?   296A

Young Socrates: Certainly.

Stranger: Do you know the account put forth by most people in such a case?

Young Socrates: I don't have it in mind at this very moment.

Stranger: Well, it's certainly plausible. For they say that if someone is familiar with better laws contrary to the ones that came from those before him, he must by all means set them down, but only after he's persuaded his city in each instance, not otherwise.

Young Socrates: Of course. Isn't that correct?

Stranger: Perhaps. And so if someone, without persuading,   B
forces the better, answer: What will be the name of the force? Or no, not yet—first answer with regard to what we were discussing earlier.

Young Socrates: What exactly do you mean?

Stranger: What if, after all, someone, without persuading his patient, practices his art correctly and compels a child, or some man, or even a woman to do the better thing, contrary to what's been written down, what will be the name of this force? Wouldn't it be anything rather than what's called "sick-making error contrary to art"? And is it possible for the one who was forced in a case of this sort to say anything correctly except   C
that he had suffered what was sick-making and artless at the hands of the doctors who used the force?

Young Socrates: What you say is most true.

Stranger: And what is the error that's contrary to the art of statesmanship to be called by us? Isn't it "ugly and bad and unjust"?

Young Socrates: Altogether so.

Stranger: Now if those who have been forced, contrary to what's been written and to ancestral traditions, to do different things that are more just and better and more

D

beautiful than what they did before, come tell me, again in respect to the blame from such people regarding such force—mustn't any one of them say on each occasion, unless he's going to be the most laughable of all men, anything but that those who were forced had suffered what was ugly or unjust or bad at the hands of those who used the force?

Young Socrates: What you say is most true.

Stranger: But are the things enforced just, if the one using the force is rich, unjust if he's poor? Or if someone, whether rich or poor, using persuasion or not using persuasion, in accordance with writings or contrary

E

to writings, accomplishes what's advantageous, must not this be, with regard to these things too, the truest distinguishing mark of the correct managing of a city, which the wise and good man will use to manage the affairs of the ruled? Is it the case that just as the

297A

pilot preserves his fellow sailors by closely guarding at all times the advantage of his ship and sailors, not by laying down writings but by putting forth his art as law, so too, in this same manner the correct regime would come about from those who are able to rule in this way, by putting forth the strength of their art as superior to the laws? And there is no error for thought-

B

ful rulers, whatever they do, so long as they guard one great thing, and, by at all times distributing to those in the city what's most just with intellect and art, both are able to preserve them and make better men from worse as much as possible—is there?

Young Socrates: It's not possible to contradict what's now been said.

Stranger: And surely we mustn't speak against those other things we said either.

Young Socrates: Which do you mean?

Stranger: That never could a multitude composed of any men whatsoever get hold of this sort of science and

C

prove able to manage a city with intellect—instead, that one regime that's correct must be sought in the neighborhood of what's small and few, even one, and the rest must be set down as imitations, just as was said a little earlier, some of them imitating this one regime in a more beautiful way, others in an uglier.

Young Socrates: How so? What's that you've said? For I guess I didn't understand that point about imitations at all just now.

Stranger: And yet it's no mean thing if someone who's set this argument in motion should drop the argument on the spot and not go through it and indicate the error that now arises concerning it.   D

Young Socrates: What error?

Stranger: Surely we must search for some such thing as this, a thing not at all familiar or easy to see. All the same, let's attempt to get hold of it. Come now. Since the regime we've talked about is in our view the only correct one, you do know, don't you, that the other regimes must be preserved by employing writings that stem from this one, doing what's now praised, although it's not most correct?

Young Socrates: What's that?

Stranger: No one among the people in the city is to dare to do anything against the laws, and the one who so dares is to be punished by death and by all the most   E
extreme measures. And this obtains most correctly and beautifully as a second choice, whenever someone sets aside what we just said was first. But let's go through the manner in which what we've called second has come about. Shall we?

Young Socrates: By all means.

Stranger: So let's go back again to those likenesses to which it's always necessary to liken kingly rulers.

Young Socrates: Which likenesses?

Stranger: The well-born pilot and the doctor who's "worth many others."[36] Let's take a look by molding a sort of figure of them.

---

36   *Iliad* XI, 514: "For a healer is a man worth many others both for cutting out arrows and for sprinkling soothing potions."

Young Socrates: What sort of figure?

298A   **Stranger:** One like this. Suppose, concerning them, that we all thought we suffered most terribly at their hands. For whichever of us either of the two wishes to save, him they save in similar ways, and whom they want to maim they maim, cutting and cauterizing and on top of that prescribing that we bring payments to them like tributes, of which they spend little on the sick man or even nothing, while they themselves as well as their B   families use the rest. What's more, after taking money bribes from relatives or from some enemies of the sick man, they end up killing him off. And the pilots in their turn bring about a thousand other such things. They leave us behind stranded because of some conspiracy when they set out; and they arrange accidents on the high seas and throw us over into the water, and engage in other evil-doing.

Now suppose, with this in mind, we resolved on some C   plan for dealing with these matters and no longer allowed either of these arts to rule at all autocratically over either slaves or free men, but collected an assembly of ourselves, either the whole people or only the rich, and enabled anyone from among laymen and the rest who are craftsmen to throw in an opinion about any sea voyage as well as about sicknesses—how we should use drugs and medical instruments on the sick, and also how we should use the ships themselves as D   well as the nautical instruments for the use of ships, and about the dangers both from winds and sea for the voyage itself and from encounters with pirates, and whether, consequently, we must fight a sea battle with ships of war against other such ships. And once we've inscribed on some tablets or stone slabs, or even set down as unwritten ancestral customs, whatever was decreed by the multitude about these matters, whether E   some doctors and pilots or the rest who are laymen join in the deliberations, then henceforth for all time to come, in accordance with this voyages are to be made and treatments of the sick performed.

Young Socrates: What you've described is totally absurd.

Stranger: And suppose the rulers of the multitude were set up annually, either from the rich or from the people as a whole—whoever happens to be chosen by lot—and that the rulers so set up ruled as pilots of ships and healers of the sick in accordance with the writings.

Young Socrates: That's even more troublesome.

Stranger: Now behold what follows after that. For when the year in office for each of the rulers has expired, we'll have to establish courts composed of men, either by a prior selection from among the wealthy or again by lottery among the people as a whole, and haul before them those who had ruled and call them to account; and anyone who wants to can bring charges against someone for not piloting the ships during his year in office in accordance with the writings or in accordance with the ancient customs of their ancestors; and these same things also hold for healers of the sick; and for those who've been condemned, the courts decide what some of them must suffer or what fine they must pay.

299A

Young Socrates: Then surely anyone who is willing to rule, and under these conditions does so voluntarily, would most justly suffer whatever penalty and pay whatever fine.

B

Stranger: And then, in addition, we'll have to set down a law to cover all the following things. If it becomes apparent that anyone, contrary to the writings, is inquiring into piloting and what pertains to navigation, or health and the truth of medicine regarding both winds and things hot and cold, or cleverly contriving anything whatsoever about such things, in the first place he will be named neither a skilled doctor nor a skilled pilot but a head-in-the-clouds talker, some chattering sophist; and then, in the second place, anyone who wants to among those permitted may draw up an indictment and haul him into this, well, court of justice, on the grounds that he is corrupting others younger than himself and seducing them into applying themselves to piloting and medicine not in accordance with

C

the laws but into ruling autocratically the ships and the sick.[37] And if in the opinion of the court he is found to be persuading either the young or the old contrary to the laws and what's been written, then he must be punished with the most extreme penalties. Nothing must be wiser than the laws, for no one is ignorant of what pertains to medicine and health, or to piloting and navigation, since it's possible for anyone who wants to do so to learn what's been written and the ancestral customs that have been laid down.

D

Now if all this should come to be just as we're saying regarding these sciences, Socrates, both in these cases and in that of generalship and every kind whatsoever of hunting as a whole, and of painting or any part whatsoever of imitation as a whole and of carpentry and the whole of tool-making of whatever sort, or also agriculture and the whole art that has to do with plants—or if, again, we should observe a certain horse-feeding occurring in accordance with a body of writings, or the entire art of herd-minding, or divination or whatever entire part service has embraced, or draught-playing, or the entire art of arithmetic, whether it's bare or plane or in things having depth or in speeds—what on earth would become apparent regarding all these things if they were practiced in this way, and came about in accordance with a body of writings and not in accordance with art?

E

Young Socrates: It's plain that all the arts would be completely destroyed for us, nor would they ever arise at a later time because of this law that prohibits inquiring; so that life, which is difficult even now, would hereafter become utterly unlivable.

300A

Stranger: What about the following? If we should compel each of the artisans mentioned to be in conformity with writings, and the one elected or chosen by lot to oversee our writings, but this man, giving no heed

---

37   The passage reminds us of the accusations to which Socrates responds in the *Apology* and which are derived, in part, from Aristophanes' depiction of Socrates in the *Clouds*.

to the writings, should attempt, either for the sake of some profit or some private favor, to do other things contrary to them, while not being at all familiar with anything about them, wouldn't this prove to be an evil still greater than the earlier evil?

Young Socrates: Most true.

Stranger: For if, I imagine, contrary to laws set down after much experience and by certain councilors who together offered some nice pieces of council and persuaded the multitude to set them down—if a man dared to act contrary to these, fashioning an error many times that of the first error, he'd overturn every practice to a still greater degree than the writings do.   B

Young Socrates: Of course he will.

Stranger: So on account of these things, a second sailing[38] for those who set down laws and writings about anything whatever is this: Never allow either one man or any multitude to do anything whatsoever contrary to them.   C

Young Socrates: Correct.

Stranger: Then wouldn't these writings—the ones that have been written by those who know as much as it's possible to know—in each case be imitations of the truth?

Young Socrates: Of course.

Stranger: And yet, if we remember, we said that he who knows, the statesman in his very being, will do many things by art with regard to his own practice without giving any heed to his writings, whenever other things seem better to him that are contrary to the things he has written and sent as orders to those who are absent.   D

Young Socrates: We were in fact saying this.

Stranger: Then when any one man whatever or multitude whatever, for whom laws happen to be laid down, attempts to do anything whatever contrary to these, on

---

38   "Second sailing" (*deuteros plous*) refers to the fallback on oars in sailing vessels when the wind fails, thus a second best way (see *Phaedo* 99D and *Philebus* 19C).

the grounds that something other is better, they do, as much as they can, exactly the same thing which that true statesman does?

Young Socrates: By all means.

Stranger: Now if they should be without knowledge and do such a thing, although they would be attempting to imitate the true, wouldn't they nevertheless imitate it badly all around; but if they're artful, isn't this no longer an imitation but that truest thing itself?

E

Young Socrates: Entirely, I suppose.

Stranger: And yet there's our standing agreement—at least we agreed earlier—that no multitude at all is able to get hold of any art whatsoever.

Young Socrates: It certainly stands.

Stranger: Then if there is some kingly art, the multitude of the wealthy and the people as a whole could never get hold of this statesmanly science.

Young Socrates: How could they?

Stranger: Such regimes, then, if they are to imitate as beautifully as possible that true regime of the single man ruling with art, must, as it seems, not ever do anything at all against the writings and ancestral customs of the laws that are laid down for them.

301A

Young Socrates: Most beautifully put.

Stranger: So when the rich imitate this, then we call such a regime "aristocracy," and whenever those who don't give heed to the laws do it, "oligarchy."

Young Socrates: Looks like it.

Stranger: And again, surely whenever one man rules in accordance with the laws, imitating the knower, we call him "king," not marking off by name the man who rules by himself with science from the one who does so with opinions in accordance with the laws.

B

Young Socrates: Looks like we do.

Stranger: Therefore, if some one man who is in addition

a genuine knower rules, he, in any case, will be addressed by the same name—"king"—and none other. That's exactly why the five names of what are now called regimes have proved to be only one.[39]

Young Socrates: It seems so, at any rate.

Stranger: What about this? When some one ruler acts neither according to laws nor according to customs, but claims, just as does the knower, "What is best, after all, must be done, contrary to the writings," and a certain desire and ignorance is guiding this imitation, then mustn't each such man be called "tyrant"?

C

Young Socrates: Certainly.

Stranger: In just this way, we affirm, a tyrant has come about, and a king and oligarchy and aristocracy and democracy, because human beings bear with bad grace that man who rules by himself, and don't believe that anyone would ever prove so worthy of such rule as to want and be able, by ruling with virtue and science, to distribute correctly the just and the holy among all, but would harm as well as kill and treat badly whomever of us he wished at any time; although if such a one as we have described were to come about, he would be cherished and, piloting with precision, would, by himself, happily manage a correct regime.

D

Young Socrates: Certainly.

Stranger: But now, since, as we indeed affirm, no king is born in the cities such as naturally spring up in beehives—a single person who is obviously distinguished in body and soul—people, as it seems, must come together to compose writings, chasing the tracks of the truest regime.

E

Young Socrates: Looks like it.

Stranger: Do we wonder then, Socrates, at how many bad things happen to come about in such regimes, and

---

39 The stranger appears to mean that there is, in philosophic strictness, only one kind of regime: kingship, which is either genuine or, in the case of the other four, imitative and derivative.

302A how many will happen to come about, when such a foundation underlies them, one that directs actions in accordance with writings and customs and not with science? Wouldn't any other art carrying on like this be manifest to everyone as ruining all the things that come about in this way? Or must we rather wonder how a city is something strong by nature? For even though cities have in fact suffered such things now for a boundless amount of time, nevertheless some among them are steadfast and are not overturned. Many, it is true, just like ships that go down, sometimes are destroyed and have been destroyed and will continue to go on being destroyed through the wretched condition of their pilots and crews, who've taken hold of the greatest ignorance about the greatest things, men who

B recognize almost nothing about political matters but think that in almost all cases they've taken hold of this of all sciences with the greatest clarity.

Young Socrates: Most true.

Stranger: So, then, exactly which of these incorrect regimes is the least difficult to live with—though they're all difficult—and which the most burdensome? Must we take a look at some such thing as this, even if in light of the subject now before us we call it a side issue? After all, perhaps on the whole we all do everything for the sake of this sort of thing.

Young Socrates: Of course, we must.

C **Stranger:** Well, then, declare that although there are three, one and the same regime proves to be eminently difficult and most easy.

Young Socrates: What are you declaring?

Stranger: Nothing but this: I'm declaring that the rule of one (or monarchy) and the rule of few and of many were the three we talked about when the present speech had first flooded in on us.

Young Socrates: They were indeed.

Stranger: Well, then, cutting each one in two, let's make six, separating off the correct one apart from these as seventh.

Young Socrates: How?

Stranger: We declared that out of monarchy came kingship   D
and tyranny, and again out of the non-many, both the
auspiciously named aristocracy and oligarchy, while
what in turn came out of the many we then set down
as simple and named it "democracy." But now, in turn,
we must set this down too as double.

Young Socrates: How exactly? And dividing it in what way?

Stranger: In no way that differs from the other cases, even if
the name for this regime now does double duty. At any   E
rate, ruling according to laws, as well as doing so un-
lawfully, is possible in this case as well as in the others.

Young Socrates: It is indeed.

Stranger: Now back then, when we were seeking the correct
regime, this cut wasn't useful, as we showed in those
earlier discussions, while once we removed that one
and set down the others as necessary, among these regimes the cut that pertains to unlawful and lawful cuts
each of these in two.

Young Socrates: It seems likely, now that this account has
been voiced.

Stranger: Monarchy, then, when yoked within good writings,
which we call laws, is best of all the six, while without
laws it's difficult and most burdensome to live with.

Young Socrates: Looks like it.   303A

Stranger: But just as what's few is a mean between one and
a multitude, so let's also regard the regime of the non-
many as a mean in both ways. And, again, let's regard
the regime of the multitude as weak in all respects and
capable of nothing great, either good or bad, as compared with the others, because the offices in this one
have been distributed in bits to many men. That's why
it has proved to be worst of all these regimes when
they're lawful, but best of them when they're all lawless. And when they're all undisciplined, living in a   B
democracy wins out, but when they're orderly, life is
least livable in this regime, while life in the first is by

far first and best—except for the seventh. For that one must be singled out from all the rest of the regimes, as a god from men.

Young Socrates: That's how this appears both to come about and to follow, and we must do just as you say.

Stranger: Then we must also divide off the men who have a share in all these regimes—except for the scientific regime—on the grounds that they are not statesmen but faction-makers and, as overseers of the greatest idols, are themselves such, and, as being the greatest imitators and wizards, prove to be the greatest sophists among the sophists.

Young Socrates: Looks like this term has very correctly twisted round on the so-called statesmen.

Stranger: Well then, this is our drama, as it were, pure and simple. As we said a while ago, a sort of procession of centaurs and satyrs was sighted, which would have to be separated from the statesmanly art.[40] But now, in this way, it has been separated, with a great deal of difficulty.

Young Socrates: It appears so.

Stranger: There remains another group still more difficult than this in being both more akin, and nearer, to the kingly kind, as well as more resistant to thorough understanding. And to me we appear to have fallen into a condition like that of those who refine gold.

Young Socrates: How's that?

Stranger: I suppose those craftsmen, too, first separate off dirt and rocks and many other things. And after this there remain, mixed together with the gold, things akin to it that are held in honor and separable by fire alone—bronze and silver, and sometimes there's adamant, too—which things, separated with difficulty by smeltings along with tests, allow us to see so-called unadulterated gold itself alone by itself.

Young Socrates: At any rate, it's said that these things come about in this way.

---

40   See 291A-C.

Stranger: Well then, according to the same account, it seems that for us now, too, things other than the science of statesmanship—all that's foreign to it and unfriendly—have been separated off, and there remains what's held in honor and akin. And among these, I suppose, are generalship and judging and such rhetoric as shares in the kingly art, which, by prompting what's just, helps pilot the practices within the cities. In what manner, then, will someone partition these off most easily and show that man who is sought by us naked and alone by himself?

304A

Young Socrates: It's plain that we must somehow try to do this.

Stranger: Then, if it's a matter of trying, he will manifest. But we must attempt to make him plain through music. So tell me—

Young Socrates: What?

Stranger: I suppose, in our view, there's a certain learning of music and, on the whole, of the sciences concerned with handicraft?

B

Young Socrates: There is.

Stranger: Again, what about the following? Shall we declare that there is, in turn, a certain science about these things that tells whether, in the case of any one of them, we must either learn it or not—or how is it?

Young Socrates: Just so, we shall declare there is.

Stranger: Won't we agree that this science is other than those?

Young Socrates: Yes.

Stranger: And which shall we agree on? That none of these must rule, one over another; or that those must rule over this one; or that this one must be in charge so as to rule all the others together?

Young Socrates: This one must rule over those.

Stranger: So then, are you declaring that this science that tells whether one must learn or not must, for us, rule over the science that is being learned and that teaches?

C

Young Socrates: Very much so.

Stranger: And the science, then, that tells whether one must persuade or not must rule over the science able to persuade?

Young Socrates: Of course.

Stranger: Alright. To what science, then, shall we give over the ability to persuade a multitude and mob through story-telling but not through teaching?

D

Young Socrates: This, too, is manifest, I think, that it's something that must be given to rhetoric.

Stranger: And determining whether one must do anything whatever to someone, by persuasion or also by force, or even whether to keep entirely quiet—to what sort of science, in turn, shall we assign this?

Young Socrates: To the one that rules over the science of persuasion and speaking.

Stranger: But that would be, as I think, none other than the power of the statesman.

Young Socrates: Most beautifully put.

Stranger: So this rhetorical ability seems quickly to have been separated from statesmanship as being another form, indeed one subservient to it.

E

Young Socrates: Yes.

Stranger: And what are we to think of this following sort of power?

Young Socrates: Which sort?

Stranger: The power of determining how one must wage war against each of those on whom we've chosen to make war—will we call it artless or artful?

Young Socrates: And how could we think of it as artless, when in fact generalship and every warring practice practices it?

Stranger: And the power that's able, and knows how, to deliberate about whether war must be made or a cessation must be obtained through friendship—should we assume this to be other than, or the same as, that one?

Young Socrates: By what followed before, it's necessary to assume that it's other.

Stranger: Shall we therefore declare it as ruling that one—if, that is, we're to make an assumption that's in fact similar to our earlier ones?   305A

Young Socrates: I declare it.

Stranger: Then what on earth shall we even venture to declare is mistress of so terrible and great an art—the art of war as a whole—except of course the art that is genuinely kingly?

Young Socrates: None other.

Stranger: Then we won't set down as statesmanly the science of the generals, since it's subservient.

Young Socrates: It's not likely.

Stranger: Come then, let's also take a look at the power of the judges who judge correctly.   B

Young Socrates: By all means.

Stranger: Does it have any power more far-reaching than, in matters pertaining to contracts, that of discerning the things ordained as both just and unjust by keeping in sight whatever is laid down as lawful and which it received from a law-giver king, providing its own special virtue, which is this: not to be defeated by any bribes or fears or pleas, or by any hatreds or friendships, so as to be willing to decide the lawsuits people bring against each other contrary to the arrangement of the law-giver?   C

Young Socrates: No, but all the work of this power is pretty much what you've said.

Stranger: Then we find that the strength of the judges, too, isn't kingly, but is guardian of laws and servant of kingship.

Young Socrates: That's likely, at least.

Stranger: So, looking at all the sciences that we mentioned,

D one must realize this: none of them at all came to light as statesmanship. For the science that's genuinely kingly must not itself act, but, by recognizing both the origin and onset of the greatest things in the cities regarding what's timely and also what's untimely, must rule those that have the power to act; and the rest must do what's been prescribed.

Young Socrates: Correct.

Stranger: Then for these reasons, since the ones we've just gone through rule neither one another nor themselves, while each is related to its own specific action, each has justly taken on a specific name in accordance with the specificity of its actions.

E **Young Socrates:** At any rate, it seems likely that they have.

Stranger: But the one that rules both all these and the laws, exercising care for all the things throughout a city and weaving them all together most correctly, we may, as it seems, comprehending its power by a term denoting what's common, most justly call statesmanship.

Young Socrates: That's altogether so.

Stranger: Then wouldn't we also want to go at it now according to the paradigm of weaving, now that all the kinds throughout a city have also become plain to us?

Young Socrates: Very much so.

306A **Stranger:** Then, as it seems, we must speak of the kingly interweaving—both what sort it is and in what manner it gives us what sort of web through its interweaving.

Young Socrates: That's plain.

Stranger: Therefore it's become necessary, as it appears, to show what is in fact a difficult matter.

Young Socrates: But for all that, it must be said.

Stranger: For the claim that a part of virtue in a certain manner differs with a form of virtue is easily attacked by those who dispute about arguments with a view to the opinions of the many.

Young Socrates: I don't understand.

Stranger: Well, here it is again. I suppose you think that
courage for us is one part of virtue.[41]

B

Young Socrates: Entirely so.

Stranger: And that moderation, at any rate, is surely something other than courage; yet this too, of course, is one
portion of virtue, of which that other is a portion as well.

Young Socrates: Yes.

Stranger: Then about these things we must dare to bring to
light a somewhat astonishing doctrine.

Young Socrates: What sort?

Stranger: That, in a certain manner, the pair of them have a
deep-seated enmity toward one another and maintain
an oppositional faction in many of the things that *are*.

Young Socrates: How do you mean?

Stranger: It's in no way a doctrine that's customary. Indeed,
all the portions of virtue at least are said, I suppose, to
be friendly to one another.

C

Young Socrates: Yes.

Stranger: Then, paying very close attention, let's look into
whether this is so simple, or it's more than anything
the case that something of them maintains a difference
with their kin in some respect.

Young Socrates: Yes, please say in what way we must look
into it.

Stranger: Among all things we should search for all those
which, though we call them beautiful, we put into two
forms opposed to one another.

---

41   "Virtue," here and elsewhere, is our translation of *aretê*, "moderation"
our translation of *sôphrosynê*, literally, "sound-mindedness." "Courage" is our standard translation of *andreia*, from *anêr*, man, male, hus-
band, but at 306 and 307E we temporarily render it as "manliness." At
306E, "manly" is *andreios*, and "manlike" *andrikos*. See Glossary under
"virtue."

Young Socrates: Speak still more clearly.

Stranger: Keenness and swiftness, whether in bodies or within souls or in movement of the voice, whether they belong to these things themselves or are present in their images—all those imitations that music and graphic art too provide by imitating—of any of these things have you ever yourself been a praiser or perceived another praising them while you were present?

Young Socrates: Certainly.

Stranger: Do you also recall in what manner they do it in each of these cases?

Young Socrates: In no way.

Stranger: Then would I be able to show it to you through speeches, in just the way I'm thinking of it?

Young Socrates: Why not?

Stranger: You seem to think such a thing is rather easy. So let's look into it in kinds that are opposed. For whenever on each occasion we admire—as we often do in many actions—swiftness and intensity and keenness of thought and body, and of voice too, we utter our praise for it by using one designation, that of manliness.

Young Socrates: How's that?

Stranger: I suppose we say first of all "keen and manly," and also "swift and man-like," and similarly "intense." And in every case, when we apply the name that I'm saying is common to all these natures, we praise them.

Young Socrates: Yes.

Stranger: What about this? Don't we in turn often praise the form of gentle generation in many of these actions?

Young Socrates: Very much so.

Stranger: So then, don't we express this by saying things opposed to what we say in those other cases?

Young Socrates: How?

Stranger: In each case I suppose we say "quiet and moderate," whenever we admire things slow and soft that are done in the realm of thinking and in deeds as well, and further, things smooth and deep that come about in the realm of voices, and every rhythmic motion and the whole of music when it employs well-timed slowness—to them all we apply the name, not of manliness but of orderliness.

B

Young Socrates: Most true.

Stranger: And again, whenever both of these in fact prove untimely to us, we change our minds and blame each of them, going back and assigning them to the opposite side by means of names.

Young Socrates: How?

Stranger: By calling things that prove sharper than is timely and appear quicker and harder "outrageous and manic," but the deeper and slower and softer things "craven and slack." And we pretty much discover for the most part that not only these things but also the temperate nature and the manliness of those opposed to it—they are looks destined, as it were, to be split apart in hostile faction—do not mix with one another in actions concerned with such matters; and further we will see that those people, if we track them down, who have these in their souls, differ with one another.

C

Young Socrates: Where exactly do you mean us to look?

Stranger: In all these things we spoke of just now and, as is likely, in many others. For I think, in accordance with their kinship to either, people praise some of these things as being of their own family, while they blame as alien other things, which differ, and they settle into a position of great enmity toward each other, and about many matters.

D

Young Socrates: Looks like they do.

Stranger: Well then, at least this sort of difference between these forms is child's play. But concerning the greatest matters, a disease occurs and proves to be the most hateful of all for cities.

Young Socrates: What sort of things are you speaking about exactly?

E   **Stranger:** About what concerns the whole management, as seems likely, of living. For those who are especially orderly are ready to live an ever-quiet life, themselves by themselves, minding their own business alone by themselves, both when they associate in this way with everyone at home and when, with respect to the cities out there, they're similarly ready to keep some sort of peace in every way. And because this love[42] is in fact more untimely than it ought to be, whenever they do what they want, they themselves slip into an unwarlike condition and dispose the young similarly, and they're always at the mercy of those who attack them. As a result, in not many years they themselves and 308A   their children and the whole city, instead of being free, often slip into becoming slaves themselves.

Young Socrates: You speak of a hard and terrible condition.

Stranger: But what about those inclining more toward courage? By always tensing up their own cities for some war, through desire for such a life—a desire more vehement than is needful—don't they settle into enmity with many and powerful people, and either utterly destroy their fatherlands or again risk making them slaves and subjects to their enemies?

B   **Young Socrates:** That, too, is how it is.

Stranger: Then how are we to deny that in these cases both these kinds always maintain the most abundant and greatest enmity and faction toward each other?

Young Socrates: In no way at all will we deny it.

Stranger: Then haven't we discovered the very thing we were looking at in the beginning: that portions of virtue, no small ones, as a pair differ with each other by nature, and moreover drive the people who have them to be in this same condition?

Young Socrates: Looks that way for the pair of them.

---

42   Love here is *erôs*, erotic passion.

Stranger: Then let's take hold of this next point in turn.

Young Socrates: Which one?

Stranger: Whether any of the composing sciences anywhere   C
willingly puts together any particular thing among its
works, even if it's the most paltry, out of some shabby
as well as good-quality materials; or does every science everywhere throw away what's shabby as much
as it can, after taking up the things that are appropriate
and of good quality, and from these things, which are
both similar and dissimilar, craft some one power and
look, gathering all of them into one?

Young Socrates: Certainly.

Stranger: Then neither will the statesmanship that for us is
truly according to nature ever willingly put together   D
any city out of human beings good and bad; but it's
very plain that it will first test them in play, and after
the test it will hand them over in turn to those who
are capable of educating them and who serve this very
purpose, while it itself prescribes and supervises, just
as weaving gives prescriptions to and supervises both
the carders and those who do all the other preparatory
work for its weave, giving indications to each of them   E
to complete whatever such works it believes to be appropriate for its own interweaving.

Young Socrates: By all means.

Stranger: It appears to me that in this very same way kingship,
retaining for itself the power of the commanding art,
will not entrust any lawful educators and nurturers with
practicing anything unless, by producing with a view to
its own blending, they achieve a certain fitting character,
and it urges them to do their educating for this alone.
And as for those who aren't capable of sharing in a courageous and moderate character, and everything else that
tends to virtue, but are violently driven off course by a
bad nature into godlessness and arrogance and injustice,   309A
it casts them out by punishing them with death penalties
and exiles and the greatest dishonors.

Young Socrates: At any rate, that's something like what's said.

Stranger: And again, those who wallow in ignorance and much baseness it puts under the yoke of the slavish kind.

Young Socrates: Most correct.

B

Stranger: Now as for those who are left—all those whose natures are capable of being settled in nobility when they obtain an education, and of receiving a mixing-together with one another with the aid of art—from these kingship attempts to bind together and inter-weave those natures that tend more toward courage (since it regards their solid character as, so to speak, warp-natured) with those that tend toward the orderly (which bring in a rich and soft and, according to the image, woof-like thread), natures that tend in opposite directions from one another, and it does this in the fol-lowing sort of manner.

Young Socrates: What manner is that?

C

Stranger: By having first joined together, according to its kinship, the part of their souls that's eternal-born with a divine bond, but after the divine, their animal-born part in turn with human bonds.

Young Socrates: Again, how do you mean this?

Stranger: Whenever the genuinely true and also steadfast opinion about beautiful and just and good things, and the things opposed to these, arises within souls, I claim that a divine opinion arises in a godlike kind.

Young Socrates: It's fitting, at any rate, that this be so.

D

Stranger: Then don't we know that it suits the statesman and the good lawgiver alone to be able, by the muse of kingship, to instill this very thing in those who cor-rectly participate in education, the ones we were men-tioning just now?

Young Socrates: That's likely, at any rate.

Stranger: And whoever, Socrates, is unable to accomplish this sort of thing—let us never address him by the names we are now investigating.

Young Socrates: Most correct.

Stranger: Well then, won't a courageous soul that takes hold of such truth for itself grow tame and in this way be most willing to commune with the just things, while the one that does not participate will veer off more toward a certain bestial nature?   E

Young Socrates: Of course.

Stranger: What about what has an orderly nature? Won't it, by participating in these opinions, become genuinely moderate and intelligent, at least, as far as a regime goes, while what doesn't commune with the opinions we're talking about most justly takes on a blameworthy reputation for simplemindedness?

Young Socrates: By all means.

Stranger: Then should we claim that this interweaving and bond in the case of the bad with themselves, and the good with the bad, never proves enduring, nor would any science employ it seriously in the case of such men?

Young Socrates: Of course not.

Stranger: And we should claim that this bond is implanted   310A
through laws for those alone who are both well-born from the beginning and nourished by customs that are according to nature, and that for just these men it is the drug provided by art and, just as we said, is the more divine bonding together of parts of virtue, parts unlike in nature and borne in opposite directions.

Young Socrates: Most true.

Stranger: In fact, when this divine bond is present, the rest, being human, are hardly difficult at all either to think up or, once thought up, to bring to completion.

Young Socrates: How so? And what bonds?   B

Stranger: The ones concerning intermarriages and child-sharings[43] and concerning private betrothals and marriages. For most people do not correctly bind them-

---

43   "Child-sharings" (*tôn paidôn koinônêseôn*) are thought by some to refer to the sharing of children by adoption, and by others to the partaking of children in the traits of both parents in an intermarriage, either when these are of different natures or from different cities.

selves together regarding these matters when it comes to the begetting of their children.

Young Socrates: Why is that?

Stranger: All that chasing after wealth and power in such matters—is there a reason why anyone would even take the trouble to blame these, as though they were worth discussing?

Young Socrates: None.

C
Stranger: At any rate, it's more just to talk about those who make their families their care, if they don't act in the right manner.

Young Socrates: Yes, that's likely.

Stranger: In fact, they don't act on the basis of a single correct reason, since they strive after the convenience of the moment and, by welcoming those who are pretty much like them, and not cherishing those who are unlike, they assign the greatest role to their repugnance.

Young Socrates: How so?

Stranger: The orderly ones surely seek out people of their own character, and as much as possible marry from among these, and in return give their daughters away to
D
them. And the kind that's all about courage acts in just the same way, when it chases its own nature, though both kinds ought to do altogether the opposite of this.

Young Socrates: How so, and why?

Stranger: Because courage is of such a nature that, if generated unmixed with a moderate nature through many generations, it flourishes in robustness at the beginning but ends up blossoming forth in all sorts of madness.

Young Socrates: That's likely.

E
Stranger: And again, the soul too full of shame and unmixed with courageous daring, being thus generated over many generations, naturally grows more torpid than is timely and in fact ends up being entirely crippled.

Young Socrates: That too is likely to happen in this way.

Stranger: These are the bonds, then, that I was saying were not hard to bind together, provided that both kinds had one opinion about what's beautiful and good. For this is the work, one and whole, of kingly weaving-together: never to allow moderate characters to stand aloof from the courageous ones, but compacting the web by means of like opinions and honors and dishonors and reputations and mutual betrothals of children as securities,[44] bringing together out of these the smooth and well-woven web we've spoken of, always to turn over to them in common the offices in the cities.

311A

Young Socrates: How?

Stranger: Whenever a need arises for one ruler, by choosing as supervisor the one who has both of these characters, but whenever there's need of more than one, by mixing together a part of each of the two groups. For the characters of moderate rulers are extremely cautious and just and safeguarding, but they lack acuity and a certain sharp and practical vigor.

Young Socrates: At any rate, that too surely seems to be the case.

Stranger: While the courageous characters in turn are more deficient than these with respect to the just and the cautious, but have vigor in their actions to a superlative degree. And it's impossible for all things having to do with cities to turn out beautifully in private and in public when these characters aren't present as a pair.

B

Young Socrates: Of course.

Stranger: This, then, proves to be, let us declare, the completion of the web of statesmanly action: the character of courageous and of moderate human beings interwoven by direct weaving whenever the kingly art, by bringing their life together into a common one by unanimity and friendship and, by having completed the most magnificent and best of all webs (so far as this life is communal)

C

---

44 "Mutual betrothals of children" (*homereiôn ekdosesin eis allêlous*, literally, "the giving out of pledges to one another)" probably refers to the intermarriage of children of heterogeneous couples. Compare Socrates' unconventional arrangement of marriages and begetting in *Republic* V.

and wrapping in it all the others in the cities, both slaves and freemen, holds them together with this weave, and, to the extent that it befits a city to become happy, by leaving out nothing that belongs to this in any way whatsoever, both rules and supervises.[45]

Young Socrates: Most beautifully in turn you've completed for us the kingly man, stranger, and the statesman.[46]

---

45 The stranger's language of wrapping everyone in a political weave sounds remarkably like what Lysistrata says in Aristophanes' comedy of that name (565 ff.). A skeptical magistrate asks Lysistrata what women could possibly do to bring an end to the war with Sparta. She responds by using weaving as a model for statecraft. The city is like a fleece that must be worked in various ways. The wool must be carded to remove those "who clump and knot themselves together to snag government positions," thus producing "a basket of unity and goodwill" that includes everyone, not just citizens but also resident aliens "and any stranger (*xenos*) who is your friend." From this now-workable wool, she says, one can weave "a fine new cloak for the people" (trans. Jeffrey Henderson, Focus Classical Library, 1988). A comedian's paradigm for a philosopher's paradigm!

46 Some editors, following the suggestion of Stallbaum, attribute this last speech to old Socrates. But, as Campbell notes, "it is not likely that [the older Socrates] would interpose without giving Young Socrates time to assent to the last proposition" (*The Sophistes and Politicus of Plato*, Lewis Campbell, New York: Arno Press, 1973 [191]). Also, young Socrates' final response echoes the interchange at 275A.

GLOSSARY

As in our previous translations, the Glossary entries are not in alphabetical order but rather in clusters of words that have related meanings. Our hope is that readers will use the Glossary not only to look up our translation of Greek words but also as an introduction to the basic vocabulary of philosophic inquiry. We encourage our readers, in addition, to consult the Glossaries that appear in our editions of the *Sophist* and *Phaedo*.

science, knowledge (*epistêmê*), **knowledgeable, scientific** (*epistêmôn*), **be familiar with** (*gignôskein*), **cognition** (*gnôsis*), **getting to know** (*gnôrisis*), **get to know** (*anagnôridzein*), **know** (*eidenai*)

Many different knowledge-related words turn up in the *Statesman*. *Technê* (see below) and *epistêmê* are the ones used most often. *Epistêmê* refers to an assured, articulable understanding of a specific subject matter—to knowledge one can stand or rest on (*epi-stasthai*). The geometry and arithmetic that Theaetetus and young Socrates have been studying are prime examples. In the *Statesman, epistêmê* seems almost interchangeable with *technê* (art): artisans as well as architects and mathematicians have *epistêmê*. In our other translations we rendered *epistêmê* as "knowledge." But because of its association here with *technê* and the stranger's emphasis on the specificity of its content, we have chosen to translate it, in all but one case (277D), as "science." We translate the related verbal adjective (sometimes used substantively) as "knowledgeable" and, in one case, "scientific" (303C).

Gnôsis is knowledge in the sense of acquaintance or recognition. It comes from the verb *gignôskein*, which can mean perceive, discern, recognize, or judge. (Our words "knowledge," "cognition" and "recognition" are all distant relatives.) We translate *gnôsis* as "cognition," the related adjective as "cognitive," and *gignôskein* as "be familiar with." The related verbal noun *gnôrisis* and verb *anagnôridzein* we translate, respectively, as "getting to know" and "get to know."

Eidenai is a third type of knowledge word. It can, but need not, refer to technical, discipline-specific knowing. *Eidenai* is the perfect form of the verb *horan*, to see, and is the source of the critical terms *eidos*, form, and *idea*, look (see below). To know, in the sense of *eidenai*, is to have seen—to be in the condition of having seen. We translate all forms of *eidenai* as "know."

arithmetic (*arithmêtikê*), **number-reasoning** (*logistikê*)

An *arithmos*—the word is probably derived from a root that means "fit or join together"—is a definite collection of homogeneous units. In other words, *arithmoi* are the whole numbers greater than "one." The artful study of such numbers and the patterns they exhibit is called *arithmêtikê*. The art of working with such numbers and the study of their relations (*logoi*) with one another is called *logistikê*, derived from the verb *logidzesthai*, which mean "reason" or "reckon" or "calculate." We translate *arithmêtikê* as "arithmetic" and *logistikê* as number-reasoning.

wise (*sophos*), **wisdom** (*sophia*), **philosopher** (*philosophos*), **sophist** (*sophistês*), **intelligence** (*phronêsis*)

In philosophic discourse, *sophia* or wisdom means something like intellectual completeness regarding the highest, deepest, and most comprehensive objects of inquiry. "Sophist" and "philosopher" derive from two different relations to *sophia*. The sophist is a professor of wisdom, that is, one who publicly claims to be wise; the philosopher, by contrast, is a lover of wisdom (from *philein*, "to love"), one who claims not to possess but to desire wisdom. In contrast to *sophia*, *phronêsis* is generally mindfulness, above all in the sense of practical or moral intelligence. We have translated it as "intelligence" and the corresponding adjective, *phronimos*, as "intelligent."

virtue (*arête*), **courage, manliness** (*andreia*), **moderation** (*sôphrosynê*), **justice** (*dikaiosynê*)

Aretê, the Greek word for virtue or excellence, has its roots in the verb *arariskô*, which means join, fasten, or fit together. Related words include *artios* (complete, perfect, balanced, even), *harmonia* (a clamp, a join, a fitting together of notes to form a scale or mode) and *arthros* (a joint or socket—think of "arthritis" or "arthropod"). *Aretê* is a kind of health or perfection or fitness of soul, an inner condition that renders one fit and ready for the work at hand. We always translate it as "virtue."

In the *Republic* and other dialogues, Socrates speaks of four virtues: courage or manliness (*andreia*), moderation or sound-mindedness (*sôphrosynê*), justice (*dikaiosynê*), and wisdom (*sophia*). It is worth noting that only the first two are treated thematically as virtues in the *Statesman*. Justice is mentioned only in passing, and in only one case is the reference (perhaps) to a virtue of the soul. And while *epistêmê*, the knowledge or science, of statesmanship, is of paramount importance to the dialogue, it is never called a virtue and never associated with a condition of the soul.

stranger (*xenos*)

Xenos means both guest and host, that is, any of two parties bound by ties of hospitality. More particularly, a *xenos* is someone from a foreign city or land, with whom one is on friendly terms and to whom one owes respectful and cordial treatment. *Xenos* in this sense can be translated as either "guest" or "stranger." The traditional rendering "stranger" captures the stranger's foreignness and also suggests the welcoming tone of the Old West greeting: "Howdy, stranger, what brings you to these here parts?" The importance of treating guests properly is indicated by Homer's epithet, *Zeus xenios*, "Zeus, the patron god of strangers."

* * * * *

speech, account, argument (*logos*)

The Greek verb *legein* ordinarily means say or speak, but its root meaning is gather or select. Hence the noun derived from it, *logos*, means everything from sentence (the weaving together in speech of subject and predicate) to account (a discerning tallying up of pros and cons) to argument (a skilful marshalling of reasons and evidence in support of a position) to ratio (a determinate relation between numbers or magnitudes). We translate *logos* as "speech," "account," or "argument," and *legein* as "say," "speak," or "mean."

distinguishing mark (*horos*)

One of the great tasks of the *logos* of the *Statesman* is to bring the statesman into view, to distinguish or bound off the true statesman from all his kin and competitors. The Greek word for such a boundary is *horos*. A *horos*, related to our word "horizon," is literally a boundary marker, separating one property from another. We translate *horos* as "distinguishing mark."

dialectical (*dialektikos*)

To become "more dialectical" is another task of the *logos*. *Di-*

alektikos, which we translate, or transliterate, as "dialectical," stems from *dia-legesthai*, literally, to "talk things through." To be dialectical is to be adept at the work of gathering and separating in speech so as to bring fundamental matters to light.

divide (*diairein*), **cut** (*temnein*), **distinguish, mark off** (*dioridzein*)

There are, in the *Statesman*, over twenty different verbs used to express the activity of division. Some appear many times, *diairein* most of all; others turn up only once. Some share common roots. For example, six different verbs are related to the basic meaning of *temnein*, cut, and *diameridzein*, *apomeridzein*, and *meridzein* all come from the important word *meros*, part. Other verbs—*diastellein, diistê-nai*—share only the prefix *dia* with other verbs and one another. Different verbs highlight different aspects of division. In some cases, the focus is on the activity of cutting or dividing (*diairein, temnein*); in others, it is on the products of the activity (*meridzein*) or the spatial separation of those products (*chôridzein*) or their number (*dichadzein, dichotomoun*) or even the activity of marking or bounding them off from one another (*diaphoridzein*). The great variety in these words and the sheer number of times they appear—over one hundred—underscore what the attentive reader notices: that dividing and separating are central to the dialogue, central, that is, to the activity of dialectic and to the activity of statesmanship. No wonder *weaving* proves to be the dominant metaphor in the *Statesman* (see below). Like statesmanship, it is bound up with a double act of separation: weaving presupposes the separating out and cleansing of the woolen mass, just as statesmanship presupposes the separation of citizen from non-citizen, while warp and woof threads, like the souls and bodies of citizens, must be kept separate in the very act of weaving them together.

Our practice has been to introduce as much consistency as possible in our translation of division words within the limits of good English. *Temnein* and its related verbs (and nouns) are translated with some form of "cut." *Diairein* is always rendered as "divide." *Meros* words always involve "part." "Separate" is always used of *chôridzein* words. But "separate" also translates *dialambanein*, and *diakritikê* is "the art of separation."

myth, story (*mythos*)

Story-telling and argument, *mythos* and *logos*, are sometimes sharply contrasted in philosophic discourse. In the *Statesman* this distinction is not so clear—its *logos* contains a great *mythos* the intent of which is, at least in part, to clarify the argument. Depending on context we translate *mythos* as "myth" or "story."

direct path (*atrapos*), **side-path** (*ektropê*), **way** (*hodos*), **pursuit** (*methodos*), **passage** (*poreia*), **make passage, make its way** (*poreuesthai*), **impasse** (*aporia*)

In the *Statesman*, as in the *Sophist*, the stranger often compares his investigation to a journey through space and time. But in the former dialogue there is an added twist: the same language is used occasionally for the motions of the cosmos. The inquirers must follow a "path" (*atrapos*) or "way" (*hodos*) or "passage" (*poreia*), avoiding distracting "side-paths" (*ektropai*); and as they "make their way" or "make passage" (*poreuesthai*), they often reach an "impasse" (*aporia*). But "passage" and "pass along" are also used to describe the cosmos, which at one point even finds itself "at an impasse." It is as if the self-reversing world were itself engaged in the give-and-take, back-and-forth of inquiry— as if the structure of dialectic were woven into the very fabric of the cosmos.

Perhaps the most important of these journey-words are "way," *hodos*, and its companion, *methodos*. Though it is certainly the origin of our word "method," *methodos* never means method in the sense of a rule-governed procedure. It is a way "after" (*meta*), a pursuit of something in particular.

* * * * *

art (*technê*), **produce, work out** (*apergadzesthai*), **to craft** (*dêmiourgein*), **craftsman** (*dêmiourgos*), **work, deed** (*ergon*), **action** (*praxis*)

A *technê* is any specialized, teachable, and publicly acknowledged know-how. What every *technê* knows how to do is generate—*technê* in fact comes from a word that means "beget" or "bring forth"—and what it generates is an *ergon*. We always translate *technê* as "art." In the *Statesman*, the activity of generating is sometimes called *praxis*, action. Two other words for this activity of *ergon*-generating contain the word *ergon*: *apergadzesthai*, which we translate (with one exception) as either "produce" or "work out," and *dêmiourgein*, which we always translate as "craft." *Apergadzesthai* can refer, in particular, to the act of filling out a sketch with color; the stranger's language and practice suggest that he regards his task as twofold: to give an account of the statesman and to paint a vivid portrait of him in words. Finally, the practitioner of an art is often called a *dêmiourgos*, a people's-worker; we say "craftsman." In the *Statesman*, as in the *Timaeus*, the maker of the cosmos is called *dêmiourgos*.

power (*dynamis*), **cause** (*aitia, aition*), **suffer** (*paschein*), **affliction, disturbance, condition** (*pathos*)

Each of the aforementioned arts and artisans, including the craftsman of the cosmos, is *able* to generate something in particular, is *responsible* for its coming into being. In Greek, to be potent or able or powerful in this sense is to have a *dynamis* (consider our "dynamite" or "dynamic"), and to be responsible is to be an *aition* or *aitia* (a word with strong legal connotations). We translate *dynamis* as "power," and *aition* and *aitia* as "cause."

In Greek mathematics, *dynamis* has a specialized meaning (see 266A-B). A square is uniquely determined, with respect to its area, by the length of its side, just as a circle is uniquely determined by its radius or diameter. A given line can be regarded, then, as a root or germ with the *power* or *potential* to "grow" exactly one square. Thus, for instance, the line that is the root—or as we say, the "square root"—of a two-foot square would be a line that is two feet *dynamei*, i.e., two feet *in power*.

The opposite of the making, the *poiein*, of the craftsman and doer is suffering, *paschein*. We render *paschein* as "suffer" and the consequence of such suffering, *pathos*, as "affliction," "disturbance," or "condition."

weaving (*hyphantikê*)

Weaving is the dominant metaphor in the second half of the *Statesman*. With this activity and its products are associated two Greek verbs: *hyphanein* (a distant cousin of our "web," "weave," and "woof") and *plekein* (related to our "complex," "duplex," "pliant," and "plait"). Both verbs already appear in Homer with the meaning of contrive or devise. Think of Penelope's web.

We translate *hyphanein* as weave and *plekein* as twine. *Hyphê* is weaving, *hyphantikê* is weaving or the art of weaving or the weaving art, *hyphasma* is web, and *hyphantês* is weaver. *Plektikê* is twining, *emplexis* is entwining, *symplokê* is either intertwining or interweaving.

The work of weaving and preparing to weave embraces a multitude of crafts and devices: the spindle (*atraktos*) and comb (*kerkis*), the warp (*stêmôn*) and woof (*krokê*), and the arts of spinning (*nêstikê*), carding (*xantikê*) and fulling (*knapheutikê*). For more about weaving, see Appendix A.

precise (*akribes*), **precisely** (*akribôs*), **be fully precise** (*diakribôsthai*)

As one might expect in a dialogue that focuses so much on arts and the importance of "due measure," words associated with precision, *akribeia*, turn up several times in the *Statesman*—three times as often as in the *Sophist*. In most cases, the word is used to characterize a failure either in the inquiry or in law. At one point, it is applied to the behavior of the cosmos! The most important, most mysterious of these appearances occurs at 284D, in the discussion of the art of measurement. In the course of claiming that the arts, including the art of statesmanship, stand or fall by the existence of "due measure," the stranger speaks of "the precise itself." The phrase seems to refer to measure as such, that is, the basis of all artful measurement—what every art looks to and participates in whenever it gets things "just right."

* * * * *

being (*ousia, to on*), **things that** *are* (*onta*), **genuinely, in its very being** (*ontôs*)

The noun *ousia* is derived from the feminine participle of the verb "to be." In ordinary Greek, *ousia* is property or real estate, above all, the homestead without which a man is nothing. In philosophic discourse, it refers to the very core of something, as in "the *ousia* of non-being." In the *Sophist*, we translated *ousia* as "beinghood"; here we translate *ousia* as "being." The neuter singular participle of the verb "to be" is *on* and the plural is *onta*. We translate *onta* or *ta onta* as "[the] things that *are*"; the italics are intended to signal that "be" means "be present." *Ontôs* is an adverb derived from the same neuter form. "Beingly" would be a literal translation. We render it, depending on context, as either "genuine" or "genuinely" or "in its very being."

form (*eidos*), **look** (*idea*), **kind** (*genos*), **shape, figure** (*schêma*)

The word we translate as "form," *eidos*, is a central term in the dialogues. Its root, [w]id (as in our modern "video"), refers to vision. *Eidos* is the form or shape or aspect that presents itself to either physical or intellectual sight; it is that through which things can be recognized. The related word *idea* means, similarly, the characteristic look of a thing, or that by which it can be known as just the thing it is. It does not mean "idea" in our sense, something that exists only in the mind. *Genos* is derived from *gignesthai*, the verb for coming to be and being born. A *genos* may refer to the members of a group who are kindred, that is, who share a common birth or generation—a tribe—or to the common character shared by those members. We always render it as "kind." *Schêma* (consider the English "scheme," or better, "schematic") is derived from a verb meaning "have," "hold", "be in a certain condition." It ordinarily refers to the characteristic condition or manner or bearing or appearance of a thing or person; in mathematics a *schêma* is a plane or solid object—circle, square, cube or cone—contained by one or more lines or surfaces. We translate *schêma* as "figure" or "shape."

generating, generation (*genesis*)

Genesis is an action-word (the "*-sis*" ending in Greek corresponds to our "-tion"). It is derived, like *genos*, from *gignesthai*, to come to be or be born. *Genesis* has four distinct meanings: the originating cause of something, the process of coming into being, the activity of generating, and the result of the activity of generating.

* * * * *

likeness (*eikôn*), **make a likeness** (*eikadzein*), **liken** (*apeikadzein*), **make a parallel likeness** (*pareikadzein*), **image** (*eidôlon*), **imitation** (*mimêma*), **imitate** (*mimeisthai*), **similarity** (*homoiotês*)

In the *Sophist*, words of imaging and imitation, of likeness and semblance, are prominent, since it is the sophist, the arch-imitator of the philosopher and the consummate maker of copies, who is being pursued. Here, as there, a "likeness," an *eikôn* (from which comes our "icon"), is a thing that is similar to an original, as a picture is to its sitter. The making of such likenesses is expressed by the verb "liken" with various prefixes, emphasizing the copying or the counterpart feature. The word *eidôlon* (whence comes our word "idol"), "image," is the diminutive of *eidos* or "form," that is, a lesser form. An imitation, *mimêma*, the product of the act of imitating, is a copy of a superior original. In the *Sophist*, a "similar thing," *homoiôma*, is a semblance, a false appearance, but here "similarity" occurs as "resemblance" in a neutral sense.

show (*deiknynai*), **indicate** (*endeiknynai*), **showing-forth** (*apodeixis*), **display** (*apophainein*), **show in addition** (*prosapophanein*), **make plain** (*dêloun*)

There are several verbs in the dialogue that have the basic meaning of "show." The most important is *apodeixis*, from *apo* (from, or away from) and *deiknynai* (to show). *Apodeixis* is Aristotle's word for logical demonstration. Here, in the *Statesman*, it has the broader meaning of showing forth or exhibiting. We translate it as "showing-forth."

paradigm (*paradeigma*)

The Greek word *paradeigma* has passed into English (and into our translation) as "paradigm." It comes from *para*, "alongside of," and *deiknynai*, "to show." A paradigm is thus something shown alongside some other thing as an example or a model by means of which the latter is made more vivid and clearer. Paradigm is one of the chief teaching devices in the *Statesman*.

* * * * *

herd (*agelê*), **nurture** (*trophê*), **care** (*epimeleia*), **tend** (*therapeuein*), **to pasture** (*nomeuein, nemein*), **law** (*nomos*)

If statesman as weaver is the dominant image in the second half of the dialogue, statesman as herd-leader or herdsman dominates its first half. (The Greek word for "herd," *agelê*, in fact comes from the verb *agein*, "lead.") Early in the conversation, the activity of herdsmen is characterized by a multitude of words from the root *troph/treph*, all of which we translate with some form of the word "nourish": *trophê* (nurture), *agelaiotrophia* (herd-nurture), *koinotrophikê* (collective-nurture), and so on. Later in the argument, a new set of words is introduced: *agelaiokomikê* (herd-minding), *therapeutikê* (tending), *epimeleia* (care), and *epimelêtikê* (care-giving). All of these new words have much broader meanings than "nurture." In fact, "care" and "tend" words turn up later in the context of weaving: cloaks, like animals, need care and tending.

Another set of related herd-words deserves mention here: the verbs *nomeuein* and *nemein* (which we always translate as "pasture"), the noun *nomeus* ("herdsman"), and the comical *pedzonomikê* ("footed-pasturing"). These words are all near-relatives of the important noun *nomos*, law, and the stranger's introduction of them is surely significant. In the Age of Cronos, when all men are herd-animals, man has god as his *nomeus* and he does not want. In the Age of Zeus, most men are needy herd-animals, and, insofar as they are, they must be guided either by a human *nomeus*—the statesman—or *nomos*, law.

city (*polis*), **regime** (*politeia*), **statesman,** (*politikos*), **king** (*basileus*)

Cognates of the Greek word for city, *polis*, turn up everywhere in English: politics, politician, policy, police, polite. They also turn up everywhere in the *Statesman*. Cities come in different shapes, with different forms of government. This form is *politeia*, which we translate as regime. (The title of Plato's most famous dialogue, the *Republic*, is simply *politeia*.) The man who has what it takes to rule a city is the *politikos*. "Politician" seems too low a name for a man of such exalted capacity. We therefore translate *politikos* as statesman and call his art or science, *politikê*, statesmanship.

Closely allied with this art and the man who has it are kingship (*basilikê*) and king (*basileus*). In ordinary Greek, *basileus* is the name for a legitimate king. An upstart ruler came to be called *tyrannos*—our "tyrant." Other types of political rule (*archê*) or mastery (*krateia*) that turn up in the dialogue include aristocracy (*aristokrateia*), the rule of the best men (*aristoi*) in a city, oligarchy (*oligarcheia*), the rule of the few (*oligoi*), and democracy (*dêmokrateia*), the rule of the people (*dêmos*).

faction (*stasis*)

As anyone who has read Thucydides knows, Greek cities were regularly subject to factional strife, often with terrible consequences—the convulsive self-destruction of Corcyra is a case in point (III.80-85). This condition of internal opposition is called in Greek *stasis*, an action word derived from the verb *histêmi*, "to stand," and related to our words "static" and, of course, "stasis." But here the word *stasis* does not mean what it means in the *Sophist*—rest. A city in stasis is not a city at rest but a city that has come to a *standstill*, a city that cannot engage in the life and motion proper to it because its parts or parties are in a *standoff*, that is, they have *taken a stand* against one another. Accordingly, we translate *stasis* as "faction."

Essay

The purpose of the following Essay is to provide a discursive overview of the *Statesman*. We shall go through the dialogue as it unfolds, calling attention to its main divisions and pointing to themes and perplexities as they arise. Readers will soon see that the Essay offers more questions than answers. One of Plato's most enigmatic dialogues, the *Statesman* is surely meant to engender searching conversation among its students, and suggestive questions seemed to us more suited to this purpose than positive answers.

I. Socrates and His Kin [257A-258B]

The *Statesman* begins with an error. It is committed by the mathematician Theodorus. After Socrates thanks Theodorus for having introduced him to Theaetetus and the stranger, Theodorus assures Socrates that he will be three times as grateful once they've worked out the statesman and the philosopher for him. Socrates, in reply, accuses Theodorus of having mistakenly treated these beings—sophist, statesman, and philosopher—as equal in worth, as though they were blank monads susceptible to the arithmetical operations of addition and multiplication.[1] Theodorus acknowledges his mistake, praises Socrates for remembering his math, and threatens to get back at him at some future time.

Theodorus' threat is part of the playful banter that sometimes goes on between friends. But at a deeper level it points to a tension between philosophy and mathematics. In the *Republic*, mathematical

---

1   The two kinds of monads or units may be called the mathematical and the eidetic, where eidetic refers to the *eidê* or forms. Whereas mathematical monads are all of the same kind, eidetic monads (like Same and Other, or Motion and Rest) are qualitatively different and require a different reckoning. For a full account of these different monads, and of the different kinds of numbers or assemblages they constitute, see Jacob Klein, *Greek Mathematical Thought and the Origin of Algebra*, Cambridge: MIT Press, 1968, pp. 61-99.

studies are essential to philosophic education: they are part of the soul's conversion from becoming to being (VII.521D ff.). To this extent, philosophy and mathematics are friends. But mathematicians, Socrates observes, dream rather than know the truth (VII.533B-C). Unaware of the limitations of mathematical thinking, they set down their hypotheses as sufficient and true without inquiring into their deeper ground in the *eidê* or forms (VI.510C-D). They fail to be dialectical. Plato's trilogy (*Theaetetus/Sophist/Statesman*) places us squarely within this confrontation between dialectic as the supreme interweaving of forms (*Sophist* 259E) and mathematics as the (nondialectical) study of magnitude and quantity.

Error is central in the *Theaetetus* and *Sophist*. Much of the former dialogue is devoted to ensuring the possibility of error, and, as we hear in the opening of the *Sophist*, the project of defining sophist, statesman, and philosopher springs from the problem of mistaken identity. Philosophers, Socrates says, are hard to recognize and appear to different people in different guises: to some as statesmen, to others as sophists, and to yet others as complete madmen (216C-D). The stranger's method of division—*diairesis*—will presumably teach us how to avoid this error. It will supply the knowledge that allows us to distinguish and thereby recognize the sophist, statesman, and philosopher by correctly matching the commonly used *name* with the rationally identified *look* (in Greek, *idea*).[2]

It makes sense that error plays a major role in the *Sophist*. The sophist, after all, deceives people (especially the young) into thinking he is wise. He is a maker of phantasms or false images (268C-D). But error is also prominent in the *Statesman*, where the stranger highlights errors of various kinds—errors of imprecision in what is said, and errors in the amount or length of what is said. Perhaps he does so, at least in part, to make young Socrates aware of the sorts of difficulties that are inseparable from the attempt to be precise about dividing kinds. In particular, he may want to make young Socrates aware of the limits of mathematical thinking, so that he may become, as the stranger says, "more dialectical" (285D).

2　After its initial mention, the mad "look" of the philosopher drops out of sight. In the *Phaedrus* (244A ff.), Socrates identifies philosophy with eros and the divine sort of madness. So why is madness missing from the stranger's attempt to solve the problem of mistaken identity? Is the mad "look" of philosophy inaccessible to the method of division? Is the stranger perhaps unwilling to acknowledge the role played by divine madness in philosophy? In the *Phaedrus*, Socrates combines what the stranger keeps apart: he calls himself a lover (*erastês*) of divisions and collections (266B).

After admitting his error in calculation, Theodorus turns from Socrates to the stranger. He exhorts him not to tire in his efforts and to choose either statesman or philosopher as the next object of his search. Theodorus and the stranger decide to give Theaetetus a rest, and so they replace him with his gym-partner, young Socrates.

At this point, the old Socrates comments on the appropriateness of moving from Theaetetus, whose features resemble his own (*Theaetetus* 143E), to the other boy, who shares Socrates' name. The emphasis on these two "kinsmen" highlights the importance of Socrates in the *Sophist* and *Statesman*. In both dialogues, the stranger does most of the talking, and he exhibits a method of division that apparently leads to knowledge. But Socrates is the one who sets the drama in motion. He is also the silent judge of what is being said. In the conversation in the *Theaetetus*, Socrates got to know his kinsman in looks. Today, after the stranger has talked with young Socrates, the elder Socrates, now under indictment, will question his kinsman in name, for we must, he says, "always get to know our kin through conversation" (258A). We are left to imagine what this conversation might have been like.

After young Socrates agrees to the plan, the stranger announces that the next man to be sought out is the statesman. The stranger and Theaetetus had divided by kind in order to capture the sophist; now he and young Socrates will do the same with the statesman. In the *Sophist*, the first question was whether the sophist was a man with an art. In the *Statesman*, the emphasis is on knowledge or science (*epistêmê*) rather than art (*technê*), though the two are closely connected. The statesman belongs in the class of those having knowledge (258B). But what sort of knowledge is this, and what does the statesman know?

II. Political Science [258B-261D] (Figure 1)[3]

In the *Sophist*, the stranger initially divided art into productive and acquisitive, making and getting (219A-C). In the *Statesman*, he divides science into the *cognitive* (like arithmetic) and the *practical* (like carpentry and the other handicrafts). Action, in this context, is a form of production: carpenters build houses, and doctors produce health.

The stranger then makes a crucial claim: so long as someone possesses the requisite knowledge, he deserves to be called by the

---

3   The Figure numbers in parentheses refer to the diagrams in Appendix B.

same name as the publicly acknowledged expert. If someone can correctly advise a doctor, then he deserves the name of doctor. If he can do the same for a king, then, even though he might be a private person with no official power, he deserves the name "king" or "statesman" (259A-B). In other words, the true statesman can be either one who rules or the advisor to one who rules. Indeed, whether or not the knowledgeable advisor has occasion to advise, he still should be called statesman because of his capacity. The stranger follows this up with another claim that expands the range of statesmanship: he attributes one and the same science to king, statesman, householder, and master (259B-C). He does so on the grounds that there isn't much difference between a great house and a small city. Rule is rule.[4]

At this point, statesmanship is classified as a cognitive science, even though its knowledge applies to the practical realm. The reason is that the statesman's power of rule has far more to do with his understanding and strength of soul than with his body (259C). This observation underscores the basis for the division within science: one form of science is manual and body-related, the other intellectual and soul-related.

But cognitive science is twofold: one part judges and leaves it at that, the other judges so that something further is accomplished. An example of the first is the number-theorist, whose cognitive activity stops once a difference among numbers is recognized; an example of the second is the master-builder, whose thoughts are put into practice by the workers who follow his orders. And so, we reach a division within cognitive science between judging and commanding (260A-B). Clearly, the statesman belongs within the commanding art, for he is no mere spectator or theoretician. Furthermore, since commands can be either someone else's or one's own, the statesman's rule is of the latter sort: unlike the herald or prophet, he gives commands that issue *from himself*.

The stranger now asserts that all rulers use commands for the sake of some generating or coming to be, and that the things generated can be either soulless, that is, inanimate, or ensouled and alive. This cut gets us closer to the king, whose power of command is exerted over animals or living things (261C-D). That is why his art, compared with that of the master-builder, is "better-born" or has a nobler origin and descent.

---

4   All of Book I of Aristotle's *Politics* is, at least on the surface, an attempt to refute this claim.

III. The Statesman and the Human Herd [261E-268D] (Figure 1 continued, Figure 2)

The stranger's high-sounding reference to nobility of birth is soon undercut by the direction he now takes. Ensouled beings are indeed higher than soulless: animals are better-born than rocks. But humans are also animals, and overseeing them resembles the overseeing of beasts.[5] Earlier, the stranger said that all rulers give commands for the sake of generating. Now he adds the word "nurture." The class we are dividing is the science of "generating and nurturing" animals (261D). This nurture has two forms: single and collective. Clearly, the statesman oversees collective nurture, the nurture of animals in herds. As the stranger comically puts it, the statesman is more like a horse-feeder or cattle-feeder than an ox-driver or horse-groom (261D).

After praising young Socrates for his indifference to the precise name for herd-nurture, the stranger urges him on by means of arithmetic: if someone divided herd-nurture in two, then he would have reduced by half the number of the beings nurtured, thus cutting our work in half (261E-262A). The stranger's formulation, which portrays *diairesis* as a purely quantitative or non-form way of dividing, may be in part what tempts young Socrates to be that someone who can reduce their work by half. He proposes that herd-nurture be divided into the nurture of humans and the nurture of beasts. The stranger praises him for his manliness or courage but also warns them both never to make this mistake again, "if it's in our power."

The mistake—the first of many—is to confuse *part* and *form*. The stranger compares this error to the mistaken division of humankind into Greeks and barbarians (262C-D). He also compares it to the erroneous division of number into two groups: the first containing all the numbers up to ten thousand, the second all the rest. It would be, the stranger says, more beautiful, more according to forms, and more in the spirit of dichotomy or bisection if one divided numbers into even and odd, and humankind into male and female (262E). The stranger's point is that a form is always a part of some more comprehensive kind, but a part is not necessarily a form. To divide properly is to find *two forms*, not one form and some indeterminate leftover. Such erroneous division makes the leftover unintelligible *and* prevents the privileged form from being rationally identified.

---

5   Compare *Cyropaedia* I.1.2, where Xenophon observes "that all who are called herdsmen might properly be regarded as the rulers of the animals over which they are placed in charge" (Loeb translation).

Judging by the stranger's response, it seems that young Socrates' mistake springs from his thinking in terms of hierarchy: humans are superior to beasts. The stranger treats this tendency as a form of chauvinism, as though Socrates is being anthropocentric and vain. He proceeds to bring *birds* into the argument, thereby anticipating the "quicker way" that will identify humans as featherless or "naked" bipeds (266E). He does so in an apparent effort to bring humans down into the realm of animals, and some animals up to the level of the rationality on which humans pride themselves.[6] What if the crane—which, the stranger remarks, seems to be intelligent—decided to divide animals into Crane and Leftover, and strutted around as though it were superior to these others, which included humans along with the other beasts! Let us be careful, the stranger warns, that this sort of "affliction" does not happen to us (263D-E).

The enormous importance the stranger attaches to the confusion of form and part in this particular case causes us to wonder: Is there a form of humankind, and if so, what is it? If we follow the stranger's admonition, then it should be possible to locate that form precisely somewhere among the other forms of Animal. Differently stated, there must be another species of some genus of animal such that the human species is defined with respect to this rationally determined other. But would finding this "other" (Bird, perhaps, or Pig?) be enough to define what it is to be human? Is it possible to define humankind solely in corporeal terms within the genus Animal, without any reference whatsoever to soul, intellect, or the divine?

The stranger proceeds to reveal another error: nurture was divided into single and collective before the animal-kind was properly divided. To correct this error, he divides animals into tame and wild and uses this distinction to guide the division of collective nurture (263E-264A). He adds that the science they are seeking applies to the nurture of tame animals in herds. He assumes that humans are tame animals that willingly undergo herd-domestication (264A).[7]

Again the stranger urges caution: they must be careful to avoid the "affliction" of having to slow down due to haste. Drawing young Socrates' attention to the tame fish in the Nile and in the ponds of

---

6   The stranger's elevation of animals to the status of "rational" continues in the upcoming myth (272B-D).

7   The stranger also seems to assume that being tame and being social or "herdy" go together. But his reference to dogs at 266A suggests that "tame" and "living in herds" do not necessarily imply each other: dogs are tame as individuals, and wolves, who are wild, live in packs.

the Persian king, the stranger asserts that collective nurture should be divided according to the two animal forms susceptible to domestication in groups: water-immersed and dry-land-based (264D). He proceeds to divide land-nurture into the nurture of winged animals and footed. This leads to the important conclusion that "statesmanship must be sought in the realm of the footed" (264E).

The stranger and young Socrates must now divide the footed-pasturing art in two, "just like an even number." There are two ways in which this can be done, the stranger says. The quicker way produces cuts of unequal size, the longer way cuts more down the middle. The stranger observes that pursuing the longer way will in fact be easier for them at this point, so that is the route they take.

They return to footed animals in herds and divide this kind into hornless and horn-bearing (265B). Clearly, the king, by analogy with other animal-herders, oversees animals without horns. The comic aspect of this division derives from the avoidance of young Socrates' earlier mistake: we cannot say "human" until it is made clear how the human kind is distinct not from beast in general but from other determinate forms of animal. So far, all we can say is that statesmanship is the nurture of hornless herd animals. To divide them, we must choose between two pairs of markers or criteria: hoof markers and breeding markers. According to the former, hornless animals are either cloven or uncloven ("mono-hoof"): according to the latter, either cross-breeding (like horses and asses) or same-breeding (like most other hornless animals). It is not clear how the hoof-criterion helps us very much, since the beings under the statesman's care lack hooves. In any case, young Socrates agrees that the statesman has care of hornless animals that breed only with their own kind (265E).

But we still cannot distinguish humans from other tame, hornless, self-breeding animals that live in herds. To address this problem, the stranger constructs an analogy that playfully connects animals and geometric objects. Humans may not have hooves, but they do have legs, and the *number* of these per human supplies a clue to the needed distinction. In the square of unit length, the diagonal is what we moderns call "the square root of two" but which the Greek geometers called the line that is "two feet in power." If we build a square on the diagonal of the first square, then the new diagonal will be the line that is "four feet in power."[8] These two diagonals produce, in playfully geometric terms, the mark by which one may separate humans from other tame, horn-shorn, self-breeding animals that live in herds.

As we take our leave of the stranger's arcane joke, we should note that the geometric definition of humans in terms of the power of two feet presents humankind as an incommensurable magnitude: there is no common measure for the diagonal and the side of the unit square. The Greeks called such a line *alogos* or irrational, since there is no ratio (*logos*) of whole numbers that describes its relation to another given line. One possible implication here is that humans are not so tame after all, and that, in addition, there is something strange about them (their erotic nature?) that makes it hard even to subsume humans under the genus "animal."

All this talk about herding animals, the stranger observes, has put humans in the same race with pigs—the most well-bred animals and the easiest to manage. Moreover, it puts the king on the same level as the swineherd. The "longer way" of *diairesis* thus seems to have ended in a joke (266C)! But the stranger prevents young Socrates from finding the joke *too* funny. Recalling the passage in the *Sophist* about the general and the louse-catcher, he stresses that *diairesis* has no care for the dignity or lack of dignity in its objects but cares only for the truth (266D).

The stranger now returns to the "quicker way" mentioned earlier and puts forth the following division: footed into two versus four, and two-footed into naked versus feathered, since humans and

---

8   The stranger's geometric joke recalls the problem Socrates and the slave-boy go through in the *Meno*—that of doubling the square (see note 9 of the translation, and Glossary entry for *dynamis*, power). The figures below show, in modern notation, the lines that represent the "power of two feet" and the "power of four feet."

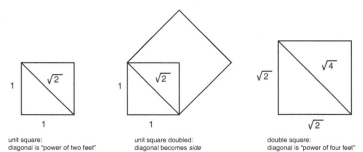

unit square:
diagonal is "power of two feet"

unit square doubled:
diagonal becomes *side*

double square:
diagonal is "power of four feet"

birds share two-footedness (266E). This last division produces the beings, now distinguished by form, over whom the statesman-king exercises his rule. But the "quicker way" does not save the result from insufficiency, for when the stranger collects the divisions of science to form a definition of statesmanship, he easily shows that, whereas the cowherd, the ruler of four-footed animals, has no competitors in his herd-nurture, the king's science, as defined for two-footed animals, is disputed by farmers, doctors, and others (267E-268C). We must therefore find a way to show forth the statesman "pure" and "alone." This way requires, as it turns out, not *diairesis* alone but a story or myth.

IV. The Self-Reversing World [268D-274E]
(Figure 2 continued)

The explicit goal of the stranger's myth is to separate the political herdsman from his non-political competitors (traders, farmers, millers, sports trainers, and doctors), thus saving *diairesis* from disgrace (268D). But the myth's enormous length and scope suggest that the stranger has a larger goal in mind, that of using this occasion to present his view of the whole of all things and the place of human life within that whole. Even so, the myth is deeply perplexing. It is not obvious why the stranger thinks a myth is necessary at all, and in what way this particular myth is able to supplement, clarify, and "save" the work of dividing by kind.

The stranger introduces the myth as a form of play, though it is not clear, as the myth unfolds, which parts are intended to be serious and which are playful. He takes this opportunity to make a personal remark about young Socrates, who is still young enough, says the stranger, for children's games (268E). The remark may be intended to correct, or at least call attention to, an excessive seriousness, or narrowness of vision, in young Socrates.[9] The stranger may also be suggesting to the math-minded youth that their recent attempt to define the human kind in static geometric terms must be supplemented, perhaps corrected, by a more poetic mode of speech,

---

9   In the *Parmenides*, the elderly Eleatic (the stranger's philosophic father) refutes and educates the elder Socrates, when he was very young. Like his namesake in the *Statesman*, he must be exhorted to engage in play in order to become fully philosophic—not, however, the play of myth but that of investigating hypotheses (*Parmenides* 135C-137B). He needs, it seems, to be less dogmatic about his "theory" of forms, more open to perplexity, and more flexible and gymnastic in argument. In the *Statesman*, the now elderly Socrates is watching, in some respects, a re-play of a crucial moment in his own philosophic education.

a mode that places human nature and human life in the context of a living, vibrant whole.

The stranger's myth may be called the myth of all myths, in that it reveals the primordial disturbance or *pathos* to which other, already-known myths refer in a fragmentary way. The stranger mentions the stories about the quarrel between Atreus and Thyestes, the sign of the golden lamb (which signified which of the two shepherds was to be king), and Zeus' reversing the course of the sun to vindicate Atreus as the legitimate king. He also mentions the time of Cronos, when people were "by nature earth-born and not generated from each other" (268E-269B).[10] The stranger bypasses the distinctly human and political aspects of these stories in favor of a cosmological overview that focuses on the great disturbance common to them all. This disturbance is the underlying cause of the alternating direction of becoming. In one epoch, becoming proceeds in the fashion of the world we currently live in; in another, it goes in the reverse direction. The life of the cosmos is a continual oscillation between these two phases.[11] As the stranger proceeds, he will emphasize the violence of the shift from one cosmic phase to the next. Indeed, the myth as a whole introduces a set of interrelated themes that will recur as the search for the statesman continues: opposition, conflict, and compulsion.

The gods play an important but confusing role in the myth. We hear about the Age of Cronos and the Age of Zeus, but it is difficult to say who these gods are for the stranger, or even how the two world-movements he describes line up with Cronos and Zeus. The stranger refers to a divine craftsman and to the gods and spirits that guide the world. The craftsman-founder sometimes seems to be different from the divine power that guides and governs, but sometimes not. The account, in any case, oscillates between two depictions of the divine: god as maker of order and god as cause of motion.

The stranger sets out by asserting that the world has two phases. In one, the god (we don't know which one) "accompanies the all as guide" and "helps it in its circling." In the other, he lets it go when the cycles have fulfilled their allotted time, and the world turns itself around and goes backwards. The reason, we hear, is that it was made by its craftsman to be both living and intelligent. Therefore,

---

10   See notes 13-15 of the translation.

11   The stranger, as we have seen, is using myth to correct a mistake in his *diairesis*. But *diairesis* continues to play a role in the myth, which draws a sharp distinction between two alternate worlds. To live in one is precisely not to live in the other.

the reversal of world-motion, though violent and necessary, is not forced upon the world from an outside source but rather happens spontaneously or from within. Reversal is in the nature of the whole. At a later point in his speech, the stranger will call this natural tendency "inborn desire" (272E).

The stranger's account of why the all goes in one direction under the guidance of a god and in another on its own goes like this. The cosmos, since it partakes of body, cannot persist in the same condition forever: it must have a share in change. But its natural motion is that of axial rotation: it moves "with a single sweep in the same spot and in the same way." Now the change that is the least departure from its natural motion is a change of direction; therefore, the cosmic animal "has received back-circling as its lot" (269E). The question is how this happens. The stranger goes through a process of elimination. The cosmos can't turn itself always, which can be done only by the divine power that guides all things; and for this divine mover to turn the world now in one direction, now in another, "is forbidden" (god cannot be changeable in his action). Moreover, we shouldn't say that two gods are assigned to two opposed motions (the gods should in no way be opposed to each other). The only conclusion seems to be that the world in one phase is accompanied by a divine cause as guide and in the other goes along on its own. During the god-guided phase, the world is rejuvenated or, as the stranger puts it, "takes on repaired immortality." The world-animal cannot by itself sustain the vitality given to it at its inception: it eventually suffers fatigue and deadening. It needs the craftsman-god to restore it to its youthful vigor.

The stranger then returns to his theme of disturbance, focusing on the moment at which world-motion goes in reverse. The violence that occurs at this time is so great that "only a small remnant of humankind is left behind." The stranger recounts the wondrous appearances of reverse becoming. At the moment of the turn, age stands still. Every living thing stops its forward movement toward looking older and then begins to grow young. The hair of elders goes from white to its former black, and bearded cheeks resume their youthful bloom. The bodies of the young grow smoother and smaller. They eventually return to their newborn state, as their souls experience a corresponding return. In the end, diminution leads to disappearance (270E).

In response to young Socrates, who wants to know what generation was like in the reversed era, the stranger recalls his earlier point that there was no sexual procreation then (and therefore no sexual desire) and that human beings sprang up out of the earth. The autochthonous race we hear about in traditional stories (which many people, the stranger says, foolishly disbelieve) has its origin in this reversal of cosmic motion.

Young Socrates asks which of these eras was under the sway of Cronos, since, as he rightly observes, a change of direction occurs in both (271C). The stranger addresses the question by characterizing life in both cycles. He says that the age in which god cares for the world, when "everything came about of itself for human beings," certainly isn't our current age. Not just one god, he says, but many—gods and spirits alike—ruled the various regions of the whole. Recalling the statesman as nurturer of the human herd, he describes these spirits as "divine herdsmen," who separated the animals according to kind—that is, engaged in practical *diairesis*—and ministered to their needs. As a consequence, no animal needed to feed on another, nor was there any war or faction (like the conflict between Atreus and Thyestes). The stranger emphasizes that in this era living things were not self-governing: "God himself as overseer was pasturing them, just as humans do now, who, being a different and more divine animal, pasture other kinds inferior to themselves."

The stranger now makes a crucial point: In this age of divine shepherding, there are no regimes and no families. There is no need of politics—indeed, no need for any communities at all—so long as gods guide the world. There is also no desire as such, since any desires that arose would be gratified without work, effort, or planning. This is the world without arts or *technai*—a Golden Age, in which fruits are there for the taking, seasons are mild, people go naked (since there is neither bad weather nor shame), and everybody sleeps on the grass. This, says our storyteller, is life in the time of Cronos. As for life in the time of Zeus, the stranger tells young Socrates: Just look around.[12]

So which life is happier, the stranger asks, the one in the Cronos-phase of world-motion or the one in the Zeus-phase? When young Socrates says he can't tell, the stranger offers a conditional

12   The stranger's reference to the Age of Cronos makes sense in light of Hesiod's *Works and Days*, which tells of a Golden Age, similar to the one the stranger describes, under the rule of Cronos. But it is not clear what it means to say that our current age is the time of Zeus. Perhaps we are meant to think of Zeus as the god of justice and in that sense the god of politics. And yet, it is odd to call this age the age of any god at all since there is no divine guidance: the Olympians do not govern.

response. If the "foster-children" of Cronos made good use of their leisure, then the people back then were indeed happier than people nowadays. In what does the good use of leisure consist? Engaging in philosophy, which here means conversing with humans and beasts, learning from every natural being its unique perception of things, thus increasing the store of human knowledge. (The rapport between humans and non-human animals recalls the intelligent cranes mentioned earlier.) Philosophy in the Age of Cronos is not the result of an erotic striving for wisdom and immortality, nor is it the result of some urgent need to order soul or city, but is rather due to what might be called interest in research: it is a peaceful untroubled "gathering of intelligence" (272C). But if, on the contrary, these people merely filled themselves with food and drink, and told stories to each other and the beasts like the ones we hear nowadays, then that too makes it easy to decide.

The stranger's discussion of happiness is odd, to say the least. It seems unlikely that philosophy, the love of wisdom, could exist in the Age of Cronos. Completely satisfied beings surely feel no *need* to engage in inquiry. They are not bothered, we must assume, by either their ignorance of the highest things or their mortality (if they are even aware of this). We are reminded that in the *Republic*, there is no philosophy in what Socrates calls the "healthy city," and that philosophy exists only where there is luxury, fever, and ornament. Even if philosophy were the gathering of intelligence, as the stranger says, it is still difficult to say why people living at that time under those conditions would want to gather intelligence. What is clear is that the stranger attributes desire (*epithymia*) of some sort, if not eros, to humans under the sway of Cronos. He suggests that the character of their desire would answer the question regarding happiness. Leaving the question open-ended, he asserts that we cannot know which life is happier until someone with first-hand knowledge, an informer from the alternate cycle, can tell us "which of the two ways people back then had desires regarding both sciences and the use of accounts." Nevertheless, the stranger clearly wants young Socrates to think about which era was happier, perhaps to get him to see that the answer is far from obvious.

The stranger pulls back at this point and recalls the purpose of the myth: to correct a mistaken division so that they can get back to defining the true king and statesman. He returns to the reverse cycle (reversed, that is, with respect to our own) and tells us that eventually the earthborn kind will come to an end. The reason is that each soul will at some point have given up all her births. At this time, the "helmsman of the all" releases the rudder of becoming and withdraws to his "lookout point" (272E), perhaps to keep an eye on how things are going in his absence. The gods, following "the supreme spirit," sense what is happening in the whole and respond appropriately. We must note here that the world does not change course because the gods withdraw their care. It is just the other way around: they withdraw their care because the world-animal, at an appointed time, yields to its inborn tendency or desire to go in reverse. What the gods and helper-gods do depends entirely on what the cosmos does.

Again the stranger returns to the theme of mass destruction. The ship of the world crashes, setting off shockwaves throughout the whole. Once again there is a universal destruction of animals, after which the world calms down as it settles into its new course. The god is no longer at the rudder, so the world must now "remember" the teachings of its craftsman and father as best it can (273B). Predictably, things go well at first, but eventually there is a forgetting and a falling off. The body, which the stranger associates with disorder, makes itself felt, and the world tends more and more toward its pre-cosmic condition. As a result, it becomes a bad caretaker and parent with respect to the animals it contains, producing effects that are "harsh and unjust." As time passes and forgetfulness becomes more pronounced, disorder brings the world to the brink of destruction. But then, the god who founded the cosmic order steps in to cure this dangerous affliction. He takes charge of the helm once more and, in effect, re-founds the cosmic order.

The stranger then goes back to the cycle in which generation, aging, growth, and nurture go on in the usual way. He does so in order to connect the myth with its purpose: "the showing-forth of the king" (273E). This current cycle, as opposed to the god-guided one, contains sexual begetting, self-rule, and politics. We should observe that, although this is the phase of animal self-sufficiency and human self-rule, an overarching cosmic necessity is at work. Sex, politics, arts, and everything else we associate with normal human life do not stem from a single persistent tendency. They belong to only one phase, where life must be what it is *because of the way the world turns*. What happens in one phase is no more "according to nature" than what happens in the other.

The stranger goes on to highlight the change wrought in humans as a result of the god's withdrawal (274B). He points out that the beasts, no longer shepherded and tamed by their guiding spirit, become violent and prey upon humans, who are powerless to stave off their attacks. Humans at this time lack all arts, including the arts of self-defense. So how did they acquire the arts they needed to survive? To answer this question, the stranger recalls stories that tell of how humans, in their state of extreme need, received fire from Prometheus, arts from Hephaestus and Athena, and seeds and plants from other deities. But this contradicts the self-sufficiency that marks the epoch in which divine care is absent, the phase in which "humans themselves needed to take hold of the course of their lives." From the stranger's point of view, the traditional stories must be false because they confuse the two opposed world-phases by interweaving divine help (the arts are a gift) with human self-sufficiency (once humans have the arts, they are god-like). In other words, the stranger's mention of the traditional stories throws into sharp relief his view that politics, which saves humankind from disorder and therefore must be counted among the *defensive* arts, exists only in a world without the guidance of gods.

The stranger ends by reaffirming the myth's cosmological perspective: Human life imitates the motion of the whole (274D-E). It cannot do otherwise. The stranger and young Socrates must now return to *diairesis* and make the myth "useful" for determining the extent of their previous error. As we now leave the myth, we should observe that in distinguishing between the age of the divine shepherd and that of the human shepherd or statesman-king, the stranger has also made it more difficult to speak of a form or kind of human beings. In particular, we cannot say, with Aristotle, that "man is by nature a political animal" (*Politics* I, 1253a8-9). "Human nature," in light of the myth, is inescapably an ambiguous phrase, since what it means to be human differs depending on which cosmic period we are talking about.

V. A New Definition [274E-276E]

The stranger recalls the double error that the myth was designed to correct (274E-275A). One error was that they confused the two cycles and treated the shepherd king "of the present circuit and generation" as though he belonged to the opposite phase: they confused the human and the divine. The other, lesser error was that, by not specifying the manner of rule, they failed to distinguish him from other human nurturers.

The stranger proceeds to revise his earlier definition of the statesman as "herdsman and nurturer of the human herd" (268C). Before doing so, he reflects on the disproportion between the figure of the divine herdsman in the myth and the king whose definition they are seeking. Statesmen nowadays, he says, are more similar in nature, education, and nurture to the people they rule. They are far from being gods. Politics is at best a shadowy image of the divine rule in the age of Cronos. But although the distinction between ruler and ruled, shepherd and flock, in our age is not so clear, the search for the true king and statesman must go on (275C).

The stranger returns to the art of giving one's own commands to animals in their community with one another, reminding young Socrates that the general term used earlier was "herd-nurture." This is the mistake that has to be fixed. The problem is that practitioners other than the statesman (farmers, for example) do in fact nurture— that is, feed—the human herd. The solution is to gather all herdsmen into a single class (so that the political herdsman can then be distinguished and identified) and come up with a name that covers them all. This new name should be "tending" or "minding" or "some other sort of care-giving art" (275E). Once this re-rigging of the name is accomplished, they can go back to earlier divisions (like footed and winged) and treat them as different forms of herd-minding. The *diairesis* would then be able to embrace the distinction in the myth between "kingship now and kingship under Cronos" (276A).

In the move from "herd-nurture" to "herd-minding" the competing claims for caretaker of the human herd are settled in favor of the king and statesman. The farmer may justly claim to feed everyone in the community, including the rulers, but he cannot claim to take care of them and to exercise "an art of rule over all humans" (276B).

Now that the class-name has been changed to herd-minding or some other, similar word, they can divide care-taking into its divine and human forms, as the myth had indicated. The stranger then returns to the manner of the statesman's rule. He divides the human art of ruling into the forcible and the voluntary (276D), thus avoiding the error of confusing tyrant and king.[13] And so, we reach our revised definition. Statesmanship is "the voluntary herd-minding of voluntary two-footed animals."

---

13   At a later point, the stranger will back away from making "forcible" and "voluntary" the proper criteria for identifying the true statesman.

VI. Paradigm, Weaving, and Cause [277A-283A] (Figures 3a, b, c)

The stranger has arrived at this new definition with the help of his "marvelous mass of myth." But he no sooner secures young Socrates' assent than he begins to criticize both the definition and the story that led up to it: the story went on for too long, and for all that never reached its proper conclusion, while the definition only captures the statesman in outline rather than in his "complete shape" (277A-C). Here the stranger echoes his criticism of the pre-myth definition. Apparently, the simple re-rigging of the name—the shift from nurturer to caretaker and minder—is not enough to fend off those who contend for the king's crown.

The failure of the myth to issue in an adequate account of the statesman and his art leads the stranger to propose another approach: the use of a model or paradigm (277D). We should note that the stranger has gone from *diairesis* to myth, and from myth to paradigm. Very soon he will take the next decisive step: he will put forth the art of weaving as the paradigm for statesmanship, since it has "the same business" (279A). But before his elaborate description of weaving, he introduces a preliminary paradigm—reading—to explain to young Socrates what paradigms are and why they are necessary.[14] A *para-deigma* is literally "something shown" (*deigma*) "alongside" (*para*) something else, and just as children learn to read by seeing complex words alongside (*para*) simple ones, so too in the case of all learning, we come to understand large and complex things, say, statesmanship, by looking at them alongside smaller and simpler ones, say, the art of weaving. As the stranger says, "the generation of a paradigm occurs" when we learn to see "what is the same"—the same letters, elements, or structures—"in something other" (278C).

The language of Same and Other recalls the problem of inter-weaving opposite kinds in the *Sophist*. This interweaving is necessary if we are to capture in speech the dialectical nature of an *image* or *likeness*—which is both Same and Other—and, by so doing, capture the wily sophist. To be sure, paradigm comes up in the *Sophist* when the stranger introduces the angler as a paradigm or model

---

14   The example recalls the paradigm of reading in *Republic* II (368D-369A), where Socrates proposes that they look for justice in something bigger—a city—in order to see it more clearly in the soul, just as if someone who wanted to read small letters from far off were to direct his gaze to the same letters that appeared bigger "somewhere else." Paradigm (in a different sense of the term) makes a striking appearance at the end of *Republic* IX (592B), where Socrates calls the city in speech "a paradigm laid up in heaven" for the man who wants to found a regime within himself.

(218D-E). But there is no elaboration of what a paradigm *is*. That the stranger dwells on paradigm in the *Statesman* suggests its greater importance for this dialogue. Indeed, given the centrality of weaving as the soon-to-be-announced paradigm for statesmanship, we may say that paradigm in the *Statesman* is the counterpart of image in the *Sophist*.[15] Paradigm and image are both dialectical in that they embody the unity of opposites and the "seeing" of Same in Other, but they do so in different ways. An image points beyond itself to a more real original, while a paradigm (as the stranger uses this term) is a learning-device that establishes a one-to-one correspondence between elements in a familiar context and the elements of something not yet known or grasped.[16] Weaving will presumably give us access to statesmanship by providing us with a detailed governing metaphor, which will teach us to "read" statesmanship as producing a whole of tightly interwoven parts or elements.

As in the case of the stranger's great myth, the treatment of weaving seems to be out of proportion to its alleged purpose, in this case, the full clarification of the statesman and his art. The main thrust of the stranger's presentation is fairly clear. The art of weaving (see Appendix A) is more or less akin to a broad array of other arts, all those that have to do with defense and protection (279C-280A). But it is even more intimately bound up with another set of arts, all those that contribute, in one way or another, to the activity of wool-working. The arts that produce the instruments used in wool-working are called *joint-causes*, and the arts like carding and fulling that work alongside the weaver to produce and maintain woolen clothing are called *causes* (281D-E). So too, we might imagine, the art of the statesman is akin to any number of other arts—all those that involve herding—but is even more intimately bound up with another set of activities that either cause or jointly cause political life, and it is precisely the latter set of arts and activities from which the statesman must be separated if we are to see him and his art clearly and whole.

---

15 Image and imitation are important in the *Statesman* as well (as we shall see in the upcoming discussion of regimes), but their problematic structure is addressed in the *Sophist*.

16 The meaning of "paradigm" in the *Statesman* is very different from its meaning in other dialogues, notably the *Timaeus*, where *paradeigma* refers not to the image-cosmos but rather to the eternal and purely intelligible original or model after which the cosmos was fashioned.

This much about the stranger's account of weaving is clear. Still, there is something decidedly odd about what might seem to be a lot of wool-gathering. For example, the stranger ends up determining the place of weaving within its kindred-arts structure twice: first from the top down (from Things Crafted to Cloaks), then from the bottom up (from Cloaks to Things Crafted). The double account, which itself seems to imitate weaving, may help young Socrates to see that structure more clearly, but it is hard not to think that if the stranger had spent more time on the first approach, the second would have been unnecessary. Again, the stranger spends an astonishing amount of time sorting out the precise relations between the various components of wool-working activity. We wonder what ultimate bearing these details of the paradigm have on the statesman's art and activity, what the one-to-one correspondence might be between the various aspects of wool working and the various aspects of political activity.

Finally, the stranger takes great pains to show that the arts of combining and separating are everywhere present, in fact everywhere intertwined, in the activity of wool-working. Combining in the form of intertwining—weaving—is only the last stage in a process that begins with separating (carding), is followed by combining (twisting), and culminates in the intertwining of threads that can only be woven together if they are initially separate. This language of combining and separating again recalls language used in the *Sophist*, suggesting that in his elaborate description of weaving in the *Statesman*, the stranger intends to illuminate not only the statesman's art but also *logos* or discourse as an "interweaving of forms" (259E).

As we leave this section of the dialogue, let us recall the stranger's main point: the art of weaving is the definitive paradigm or governing metaphor for the art of statesmanship. But the stranger has not yet said what this means. *Why* is statesmanship like weaving, and what are the threads it weaves?

VII. The Measuring Art [283A-287A] (Figure 4)

The ensuing discussion of measurement, as we shall see, sheds light on the complex account of weaving in the preceding section. It has an auspicious beginning. The stranger notices what we have noticed: he voices his concerns about the apparently excessive length and the over-elaborateness of his account of weaving, a concern he broadens a bit later (286B-C) to include his myth as well as his account of non-being in the *Sophist*. He then sets out to explain why his account of weaving "went around in a circle, vainly marking off a great many parts," that is, why it had to *appear* "needlessly long-winded" (283A-C).

The art of measurement, the stranger argues, must be divided in two. One part includes the very arts that young Socrates and Theaetetus have been studying with Theodorus. It comprises "all arts that measure number and length and depth and breadth and swiftness in relation to their opposites" (284E). All of these deal with the great and the small "in relation to one another" (283E). The other part (which includes weaving and statesmanship) comprises the arts that deal with the great and small "in relation to due measure" (283E). Such arts, all those that "produce good and beautiful things" (284B), may occasionally employ the first sort of measurement (think of the carpenter carefully cutting planks of a certain length), but to deny the independence of the second part would entail the destruction "of the arts themselves and all their works" (284A).

In stressing the need for an art of due measure, the stranger draws a provocative parallel with his account of non-being in the *Sophist*. Just as in that discussion, the stranger and Theaetetus "compelled non-being to *be*," so too the stranger and young Socrates must compel "the more and the less" to be measured by due measure and not by each other alone (284B-C).

The language of compulsion suggests that "the more and the less" is resistant to due measure, and that what might be called the law of due measure must be enforced. It is striking that the stranger compares the generation of due measure within the realm of the more and the less to the notoriously problematic being of non-being. He may be suggesting that the two problems—that of non-being in the *Sophist* and that of due measure here in the *Statesman*—must be connected. The former found its solution in the identification of non-being with otherness (257B). This allowed the stranger to account for why discourse is an articulate interrelating—an interweaving—of opposite forms like Same and Other. Due measure continues the stranger's attempt to clarify logos or philosophic discourse. Speech that aims at truth must indeed be articulate, and for that it needs the power of non-being as otherness. But it also needs to participate in the "just right" or due measure—in "the good" understood as "the precise." This is, as it were, the statesmanly character of truth-revealing speech. The stranger's emphasis on the excessive length of his own speech calls young Socrates' attention to this need for statesmanlike judgment or wisdom in the search for truth.[17] Perhaps, in the end, the problem of establishing due measure or "wisdom" within the unstable practical realm of the more and the less—the central problem of statesmanship—is in fact just as difficult as the problem of non-being!

The distinction between two types of measurement makes sense. After all, the gauge of a true artisan is his ability to measure everything he does with a view to what is fitting, timely, and needful. It is also useful as an invitation to think about the due measure the statesman aims at and what its analogue in weaving might be. As suggested above, the stranger's elaborate account of a twofold art of measurement makes sense as a response to the charge of excess if the stranger himself is practicing an art that belongs to the second category, an art that apparently generates excess in order to highlight the need for due measure as a criterion for truthful speech. In any case, the division of measure into its two forms combines with the paradigm of *reading* (to which the stranger returns at this point) to produce the most dramatic assertion in the dialogue. The stranger prompts young Socrates to agree that, just as learning to read a given word is not for the sake of the word itself but for learning to read in general, so too the whole search for the statesman has been less for the sake of finding the form itself of the true statesman than for becoming "more dialectical about all things" (285D), and especially "bodiless things, since they're most beautiful and greatest" (286A).

The stranger's explicit reference to dialectic sheds light on why he took a double approach to the art of weaving: it was apparently to give young Socrates exercise in thinking through the dialectical interweaving of arts involved in the production of woolen cloaks. It also explains why what seemed at first to be an over-elaborate account of weaving echoed the deepest moments of the *Theaetetus* and *Sophist*. "No one in his right mind," says the stranger, "would be willing to hunt down the account of weaving for the sake of weaving itself" (285D). But weaving makes perfect sense as a paradigm for dialectic. The stranger's apparent excess (in both length and complexity of speech) stems, it seems, from his attempt to initiate young Socrates—as his teacher, the elder Parmenides, had initiated young

---

17   It may be especially important for mathematically minded students of Theodoros to have this point brought home to them. Recall the error with which the *Statesman* begins. Only now are we in a position to grasp its full meaning: In treating sophist, statesman and philosopher as homogeneous units, Theodoros, the geometer, had failed, characteristically, to distinguish between the mathematical art of measurement and the art of due measure.

Socrates' namesake once long ago—into the practice of dialectic.

As was mentioned earlier, the projected trilogy of the *Sophist*, *Statesman*, and *Philosopher* begins with the elder Socrates' observation that philosophers sometimes appear as statesmen and sometimes as sophists. There are several indications in the *Sophist* that the stranger agrees with Socrates about this point, and that he means his audience to glimpse the philosopher in or behind the image he presents of the sophist. But philosophers make their appearance as statesmen too. It is likely, then, that he is giving us a second glimpse of the philosopher—as well as his objects and activity—in the *Statesman*, and that the philosopher is most visible here, at the very center of the dialogue. Taken at face value, the presentation of weaving goes on far too long. But in showing us a paradigm for philosophy, it may be of just the right length—it may indeed be an embodiment of "due measure" and "the precise itself."[18]

VIII. Arts in the City [287B-291C] (Figure 5)

The discussion of weaving revealed that productive arts require proper instruments, which must be produced by other, subordinate arts. The weaver is the *cause* of the resultant weave, and the arts that produce his threads and instruments are *joint-causes* (281D-E). Weaving, as we know, is our paradigm for statesmanship (279A-B). And so, if we want to find the statesman pure and alone, we must distinguish his master-causality from all the other arts that minister to it—as we did for weaving. Some of these do not vie with kingship; others do. The stranger goes through both kinds: the non-contending and the contending arts.

The statesman has already been separated off from other herdsmen. Now he must be separated from other contenders (287B). The stranger here indicates that they must depart from division into two. The arts, he says, must be divided "limb by limb, like a sacrificial animal"—if not into two, then into the number closest to two (287C).

Taking his cue from the discussion of weaving, the stranger asserts that all arts that produce an instrument or tool are to be classed as joint-causes. Without these subordinate but necessary arts, he observes, there would be neither city nor statesman (287D). A city requires many things, things not needed in the apolitical Age of Cronos. At first, it seems that we can call all useful things tools. But then

---

18   It is nevertheless important to ask whether philosophy and dialectic mean the same thing for the stranger that they do for Socrates.

the stranger, speaking more precisely, distinguishes tool in the strict sense—an instrument used to make something—from things that are useful in other ways.

The stranger goes through a list of seven kinds of useful things provided by various arts: tools, containers (which do not craft a thing but rather keep it safe), bearers (chairs), defenses (houses and clothes), playthings (decorations, music, and paintings), raw materials (metals, bark, and animal hides), and nurture, which provides things that tend the body, like food, exercise, and healing. Perhaps most interesting is the "first-born" form that raw materials receive before being handed over to the crafting arts. This art of pre-formation reminds us that all art begins with nature or non-art, and that the arts are not individually autonomous: each depends on other arts. The city, in other words, is not a mere collection of arts but an interweaving.

The list of seven kinds seems to cover all the things a city must acquire if it is to be a city—that is, in addition to tame animals (289A). At this point, the stranger readjusts his list so that the acquisition of raw materials comes first, followed by tool-making and the rest. He then observes, curiously, that certain things that seem to belong to no definite kind, like coins and seals, must be forced into one or another of the canonical seven (289B).[19] As for the city's acquisition of *living* things, the stranger observes that herd-nurture, which has already been divided, will accommodate all tame animals—that is, with the exception of slaves (289A-C).

The reference to slaves points to the city's need for living tools that act rather than produce. This class embraces slaves and servants (289C). The stranger, apparently acting as a sort of prophet, "divines" that somewhere in this class he and young Socrates are likely to find those who contend with the true king, just as previously spinners and carders contended with the weaver. He first goes through four kinds of servants who are easy to separate from the true king: slaves (who are the "greatest servants" and have no pretensions to kingship), traders, heralds, and scribes. He then takes young Socrates higher up the ladder of privilege to servants who, in their arrogance, do contend with the true king: diviners, priests, and kings-by-lot, that is, rulers who are chosen to conduct religious events (290C-E). These three claim some connection with the gods and thus seem to be above a mere king. The stranger's emphasis on

---

19   Again we see the theme of compulsion arise, this time just before the introduction of slavery.

pride in this section of the dialogue recalls the passages in the *Sophist* and *Statesman* mentioned earlier, where the stranger excludes from his accounts any distinction based on dignity. Indeed, his earlier reference to divining and his comparing division of the arts to the carving of a sacrificial animal (287C) suggest that *diairesis* rather than religious sacrifice is our genuine bridge to divine truth, and that the scientific approach to "cutting" is intended to expose and counteract the unwarranted pride of place that afflicts diviners, priests, and kings-by-lot. In other words, the stranger means to expose pretenders not only to kingship but also to an exalted, privileged science that contends with the genuine science of division.

The separation of these various kinds of servants, the stranger observers, causes "a very large mob" to show itself (291A). It consists of all those in cities who claim to be statesmen simply because they wield political power—the conventional rulers and politicians. They look like animals of all sorts: lions and centaurs, satyrs and "weak beasts of many wiles," who magically exchange their shapes and powers (291B). They constitute the bizarre kind "that of all sophists is the greatest wizard and the one most experienced in this art [of deception and transformation]" (291C). The sophist—or rather, the sophistical nature—thus makes an explicit appearance in the realm of statesmanship. It is from this imitator, the *sophist-statesman*, that those who are "statesmanly and kingly in their very being" must, above all, be separated.

IX. The Correct Regime [291D-293E] (Figure 6)

In order to separate the true statesman from mere politicians, the stranger turns from causes to types of regime. He starts out by distinguishing three kinds: monarchy (rule of one), oligarchy (rule of the rich few), and democracy (rule of the people, the many). Regimes are then divided according to the character of the rule: whether it is forcible or voluntary, whether the poor or the rich are involved, and whether the regime is lawless or obeys laws. These considerations expand the list to *five*: tyranny and kingship, oligarchy and aristocracy, and democracy (which retains the same name in whatever way the multitude rules).

But these divisions fail to provide the criterion for determining whether a regime is correct or incorrect (292A-B). The stranger reminds young Socrates that kingship was agreed to be "a certain judging and supervising science" that ruled over animals. This and this alone—the presence or absence of scientific supervision—is the decisive mark by which we can recognize whether a regime is correct or incorrect. But in which of the previously mentioned regimes is this science, which is "the hardest and greatest to acquire," to be found? Until this question is answered, we will not be able to separate "the intelligent king" from his sophistical pretenders (292D).

The stranger's reference to difficulty, greatness, and intelligence makes it easy to eliminate democracy. After all, there aren't many topnotch draught-players in a city, let alone kings (292E)! The stranger then recalls one of his most important teachings: that true kingship is a matter of science and has nothing to do with whether or not one actually rules (292E-293A). Since genuine knowledge is the sole criterion, the elimination of democracy does not guarantee that correct rule is determined by the smallness of the number of rulers.

The stranger then spells out the implications of this view of politics. Whether the few scientific statesmen rule willing or unwilling subjects, whether in accordance with laws or without laws, whether they are rich or poor—none of this matters "so long as they supervise by means of art" (293B). The statesman's supervisory art, says the stranger, is analogous to that of the doctor, who sometimes uses painful means to heal our bodies. What makes the doctor a doctor has nothing to do with his patients' willingness or unwillingness to submit to his remedies, or whether his advice is documented in an authoritative text. The only mark of his being a doctor is the supervisory science that succeeds in making our bodies healthier. The same holds for the scientific kings, who, like the doctor, must sometimes use extreme measures to heal the body politic (293D-E).

These rulers in the precise sense, the stranger says, use "science *and the just*" (293D). It is unlikely that justice here refers to some virtue that must be added to science. Rather, "the just" appears to mean "the correct," or what is "just right for the common good." But this makes us wonder more broadly about what the stranger thinks of justice: Is it just to force citizens to do *whatever* the statesman knows to be correct? Does freedom count for nothing? What would we think of a doctor who used force rather than persuasion to get his patients to take his advice, who treated his patients as though they were slaves? The stranger's allowing for this possibility reminds us that, early in the account, there was a single science for the statesman, the householder, and the master (*despotês*) (259B-C). In any case, the correct regime, the stranger concludes, is the one based on science, and all other regimes are its imitators—including those with good laws (293E).

X. The Critique of Law [293E-299E]

Young Socrates balks: he finds ruling without laws hard to swallow, perhaps especially because of the violence the stranger associates with it. The stranger acknowledges that "in some manner... lawgiving belongs to the kingly art" (294A), and a bit later he will become a qualified defender of law. But his first response to young Socrates' objection is a vigorous attack on the rule of law. His chief claim is that "the best thing" would be for "the kingly man with intelligence (*phronêsis*)" to rule rather than the laws (294A).

The first stage of the critique focuses on the sheer variety of human things. Because they are universal, laws cannot possibly take that variety into account. Instead, law is a crude attempt to say what is best or appropriate for a whole group of human beings. Laws have come into being for the same reason that group training sessions for athletes have—there is simply no time to do "one-on-one detailed work" with everyone (294D-E). In short, laws are deficient because they fail to focus on the particular; they lack "precision" (variants of the word are used three times in this section).

It is hard to know what conclusions we are to draw from this critique. Laws certainly lack precision; they aren't meant to have it. But the stranger's admission that *no one* would be "up to prescribing what's appropriate *with precision*" throughout each person's life seems to undercut not just law but the very possibility of politics. Does the stranger mean to suggest that even political rule *without* the mediation of law is not a human possibility, that the political art can be practiced only in one-on-one encounters with other human beings—like the political art of the elder Socrates?[20] What *is* the proper sphere of kingly intelligence or *phronêsis*?

The second stage of the critique is less harsh. Here the focus is on the variability of human things. It might make sense, the stranger argues, for a doctor or trainer, about to absent himself from his charges for some time, to leave written prescriptions. But it would be ridiculous for him to insist that these be followed to the letter under all future circumstances. So, too, in the case of the lawgiver, it would be laughable if he "or someone else like him" were not to be allowed to alter laws for the better as the situation dictates (295E-296A).

---

20 In the *Gorgias*, Socrates makes a point of distinguishing his inquiry from that of the law courts: unlike the latter, he is interested only in the "vote" of the individual with whom he is conversing (474A-B, 475E-476A). In the same dialogue, he claims that he is the only one in Athens who attempts to practice the art of true statesmanship (521D).

Again, it is hard to know what we are to conclude here. But law as such does not seem to be the problem; the unwillingness to change laws in changed circumstances is. Indeed, the stranger's extended analogy invites us to think of the statesman as either a lawgiver or as someone who, in different circumstances, could alter laws for the better. Perhaps the most characteristic use of the statesman's art is to be found not in the lawless rule of human herds but in the laying down of suitable laws or in the precise discernment of defects and possible improvements in laws already existing.[21]

The issue of changes in laws leads naturally to the question whether the persuasion of the citizen body should be a condition for such change (296A ff.). Young Socrates at first appears to think so. The stranger does not. He argues forcefully that force is a non-issue, that consent of the governed has no weight—that in fact none of the conventional criteria by which statesmen are judged are anything but external measures. The only thing that matters is that intelligent rulers accomplish "what's advantageous" (296E), that they distribute "what's most just with intellect and art," "preserve" the citizens, and "make better men from worse" by "putting forth the strength of their art as superior to the laws" (296E-297B). This last phrase confirms what the stranger had said much earlier: that the statesman rules not primarily through physical force but by virtue of his "understanding" and "strength of soul" (259C). In making or overcoming or adjusting laws, the true statesman must "realize" and make apparent the power of his thought.

The final stage of the stranger's critique of law is also a preparation for its defense. It is intended to show how the rule of law has come about and to show that all regimes other than the correct one are imitations of it, while their written laws "stem" from that one. It is less an argument than a vivid portrayal of the ridiculous consequences of abiding in all cases by written laws and public opinion. As before, the arts of medicine and piloting serve as models. Perhaps the most curious and instructive moment in the stranger's portrait comes when he imagines the person who dares to inquire into the laws of medicine or piloting being accused of being a sophist, hauled into court (on the grounds of corrupting the young), and punished "with the most extreme penalties" (299C). The description fits the

---

21　We see an instance of this art in the *Laws*, when Plato's other stranger—an Athenian this time—shapes a new set of laws to suit existing circumstances in Cretan customs and character.

elder Socrates, who is about to be put on trial, and is currently right in front of the stranger.[22]

But the stranger may be engaged in more than playful image-making. He may also be showing us how that "someone else" who is capable of practicing the true political art might arise within a law-governed imitation of the correct regime. A city open enough to allow inquiry into its foundations, and thus willing to tolerate the emergence of political philosophy, might give rise to a man able to alter the laws so as to bring the city into the closest possible accord with the correct regime.

XI. Law Revisited [300A-303C] (Figures 7, 8)

The rule of law, especially written law, may be problematic. But what would happen if there were written laws formulated on the basis of "much experience," and then someone in charge should ignore them for personal profit? Wouldn't that be even worse than trying to capture political wisdom in writing in the first place? To address this greater error, the stranger relaxes somewhat his critique of law and recommends a "second sailing" (a phrase that refers to the use of oars when the wind fails). This consists in a strict adherence to the laws, even though these are only imitations of the truth (300A-C). The true statesman will rule by his own science and give no heed to written prescriptions, while the non-scientific regimes will imitate him—well if they observe established law and custom, badly if they do not.[23]

Again, neither the wealthy few nor the multitude get hold of statesmanly science, and so their corresponding regimes, if they are to imitate true kingship "as beautifully as possible," should rule in strict accordance with the laws and traditions. Thus, the lawful rule of the rich is called aristocracy, the lawless oligarchy, while the single ruler is called king, whether he has science or not (301A-B). In this way, the stranger asserts, since all regimes are what they are in relation to the rule of the scientific king, their five names reduce to only one: "kingship." Earlier, the stranger listed five regimes (291D-292A). That was before he introduced science as the decisive criterion. But now, although there are five names, the number of regimes

---

22   A reference to Socrates also came up in the *Sophist* (230C), when the sophist turned up as the man who used refutation to purge people of "their big and stiff opinions about themselves."

23   The distinction between good and bad imitations of true kingship recalls the division of image-making in the *Sophist* between the making of proportionate likenesses and that of deceptive phantasms (235D-236C).

has grown to *six*: tyranny (lawless kingship), true kingship, lawful kingship, oligarchy (lawless rule of the few), aristocracy (lawful rule of the few), and democracy (see Figure 7).

The stranger puts "tyrant" at the head of the list (301C), noting that the rule of one man rankles human beings and causes them to despair of a king who would rule "with virtue and science." If such a king did in fact appear, the stranger says, he would be cherished. And so, in their despair and ignorance of the true king, and their bitter experience of tyrants, people are compelled to formulate laws as the only saving grace of cities. They do so because a city is not like a beehive: there is no naturally designated ruler who springs up among the inhabitants. This fact leads the stranger to revisit his critique of law. No wonder cities without scientific rule fall victim to all sorts of evils! Stressing his view that politics is an art like other arts, the stranger asserts that if any other art based its actions on written rules, the bad results would be "manifest to everyone." Then again, maybe we should marvel that a city is "something strong by nature," and that conventional cities have endured for so long in spite of artless rule. Nevertheless, the stranger mordantly observes, many do go down like ships with bad pilots and crew, who think they have perfect knowledge of the sailing art but in fact are abysmally ignorant (302A-B).

The stranger's "second sailing" leads to an important practical question: Which of the incorrect regimes is least difficult to live with, and which most burdensome? To answer this question, the stranger now divides the regimes (which formerly were six in number) into seven by doubling democracy into lawful and lawless. Of these seven, monarchy with law is best, without law worst; oligarchy is a mean between best and worst; and both types of democracy are weak—worst when compared to the other lawful, orderly types, but most livable among regimes when all are lawless and undisciplined (302E-303B). The seventh type is singled out as a god from men: the regime of the true king ruling alone (303B) (see Figure 8).

Having completed his account of regimes, the stranger now returns to the kind of politicians we find in them. Returning to his charge of sophistry, he says that these are not statesmen at all but rather "faction-makers" and "the greatest sophists among the sophists" (303C). In other words, all rulers in all conventional regimes, even the ones we might regard as legitimate and worth living in, are shams. Young Socrates strongly approves of the term "sophist," which, he notes, "has very correctly twisted round on the so-called statesmen."

XII. Rivals of the King [303C-305E] (Figure 9)

The stranger recalls the "procession of centaurs and satyrs" described earlier (291A-C). These hybrids are the sophistical regimes that have just been separated off from the regime based on science. But the work of separation must go on: the stranger and young Socrates must now be like refiners of gold who resort to fire in order to extract gold "all by itself" and separate it from other precious metals (303E). The statesman must be separated from the honored professionals who cling to him most closely. These include the general, the judge, and the rhetorician.

To show the statesman "naked and alone by himself," the stranger and young Socrates consider the various arts, starting with music and other handicrafts. These arts dictate *what* is to be learned in each case but not *whether* the art should be learned. This belongs to another science. And since no one handicraft dictates whether another should be learned, there must be a ruling science other than all these arts taken together.

What holds for the handicrafts also applies to rhetoric, which teaches us how to persuade but does not determine whether we should do so on a given occasion. This determination belongs to statesmanship. Rhetoric is therefore distinct from statesmanship and subservient to it (304D-E). So too for the general's art, which knows how to wage war but does not determine whether, in a given case, war should be made or peace should be sought. This belongs to "the art that is genuinely kingly" (305A). Like rhetoric, the general's art is subservient to that of the statesman. The same holds for judges, whose sphere is limited to guarding the laws. It too is subservient to kingship (305C).

The task of refining thus reaches its end: statesmanly gold has been separated off from its kindred metals. The stranger here emphasizes that, just as none of these alloy-arts can claim to be the science that rules them all, so too the ruling science cannot be any of these arts: "For the science that's genuinely kingly must not itself act." This assertion recalls the very first *diairesis*, according to which statesmanship was a cognitive rather than practical science (259C-D). The statesman's art, by virtue of its non-acting supervising cognition, rules over the arts "that have the power to act" (305D).

The reason why the subordinate offices within the city all have different names thus comes into view: each is related only "to its own specific action." And the science that rules them and exercises its care throughout the whole city or *polis* most justly deserves a name that expresses this communal care: *politikê* or statesmanship (305E). At this point the stranger returns to the paradigm of weaving. Statesmanship, he says, takes hold of the subservient offices within the city and weaves them together "most correctly." But political weaving, as we soon discover, is not confined to the interlacing of offices.

XIII. Virtue Against Virtue [305E-308B] (Figure 10)

Now that all the kinds throughout the city have been laid bare, the stranger presses for more clarity about "kingly interweaving." What is the manner of this interweaving, and what sort of web does it produce? This question has been left hanging ever since the stranger first put forth weaving as the paradigm for statesmanship.

This final stage of the discussion takes up "a difficult matter" concerning virtue. Contrary to what is suggested in other dialogues, virtue, for the stranger, is not a harmonious whole. Parts of it—courage and moderation—are at variance with each other (306A). The stranger puts this in the strongest terms. Now giving full rein to the themes of violence and conflict, which first came up in the myth, he exhorts young Socrates to join him in daring to proclaim that courage and moderation are "very hostile to one another" and produce faction "in many of the things that *are*" (306B). This harsh view, he says, goes against the customary depiction of the virtues as mutual friends. Throughout this concluding part of the dialogue, the stranger never asks Socrates' question: What is virtue? He deals only with the opposition mentioned above and how kingly interweaving overcomes it. This opposition, along with the stranger's reference to "the things that *are*," recalls the definition of non-being as "the opposition of being with being" in the *Sophist* (257E). The present context perhaps suggests that the political realm especially is the locus and manifestation of non-being as antithesis.[24]

To show the truth of his claim that parts of virtue are mutually opposed, the stranger urges young Socrates to consider movements we call beautiful for opposite reasons. He points to examples in musical performance, visual art, athletics, speech, and thought.

---

24   The elder Socrates is no stranger to opposition. Witness the opposition of the rational and irrational parts of the soul in the *Republic*, or, more generally, Socrates' fondness for revealing contradictions in the opinions of his interlocutors, not to mention his frequent opposition to what his city finds praiseworthy. But the Eleatic stranger seems even more eager to see opposition and tension everywhere, to look at the eidetic and political realms alike through the lens of antithesis. He may be officially a follower of Parmenides, but he sometimes seems to be more devoted to the back-stretched bow of Heraclitus (Fragment 51).

We praise movements that are keen and swift, whether of bodies or of souls, by saying that they exhibit "manliness," which in Greek is also "courage" (*andreia*) (306E). But we also praise the "gentle generation" in the smooth and slow movements of thought and deed by calling them "quiet and moderate" (307A). These subdued and measured motions exhibit, we say, not manliness or courage but orderliness or decorum (*kosmiotês*). Yet we also *blame* both sorts of attributes when they appear out of place and untimely. The inappropriately quick or sharp we call "outrageous and manic," and the inappropriately slow and smooth "craven and slack." It is clear, then, that we praise and blame movements for exactly opposite reasons, and that moderation and courage oppose each other. Moreover, this very opposition occurs in the souls of human beings (307C). Moderate people welcome their like and reject their opposite; courageous or manly people do the same. The attachment of both to their own kind, the stranger says, breeds enmity for what is opposite in kind.

But this enmity, bad as it is, is child's play compared with the much more serious disease that the mutual repulsion of courage and moderation breeds in cities (307D). People who are by nature disposed to orderliness and a quiet life want peace at any cost. Their pacifism is, paradoxically, a form of passion—*eros* (308A). Left to their natural bent, they grow unwarlike and make their children unwarlike. In time, the whole city is at the mercy of its enemies and is enslaved. People inclined to courage bring about a similar evil through the opposite cause. Their spiritedness drives them to keep their city continually itching for war. Eventually, the city is defeated by powerful enemies and is either destroyed or enslaved. What greater proof could there be that "these kinds always maintain the most abundant and greatest enmity and faction toward each other"![25]

The political problem, as the stranger here presents it, is the unchecked drive in virtuous individuals for homogeneity and the corresponding drive against heterogeneity or otherness. This drive in the soul is grounded in the antithetical natures of courage and

---

25 The opposed human kinds—the courageous and the moderate—seem to be the political equivalent, or even expression, of Motion and Rest, as taken up in the *Sophist*. Courageous individuals are always on the move toward conflict, and moderate individuals just want things to stay the same. The stranger's account of courage and moderation is in sharp contrast with what Socrates says in *Republic* IV, where "political courage" is the preservation of right opinion about what is terrible and what is not (430B-C), and moderation is the virtue that stretches throughout the whole of the city, like the tuning of a musical scale, and produces unanimity (432A).

moderation. Some people are, as it were, possessed by the one virtue, other people by the other. This drive to one-sidedness, in the stranger's account, produces the broader homogeneity that characterizes and infects the city at large. Indeed, the stranger seems so intent on stressing the dangers of homogeneous individuals and homogenous cities (with respect to virtue) that he bypasses an account of civil war and proceeds to the evils that result from war *between* cities. This even though he describes the tension at the heart of virtue as "faction" or *stasis*. On the stranger's analysis, the greatest danger that besets cities, in other words, is not faction or party strife per se, otherness in its most terrible form, but the eventual take-over of the city by a single virtue—the fanatical avoidance of otherness.

XIV. The Web of Statesmanship [308B-311C] (Figure 11)

Having secured young Socrates' agreement, the stranger focuses on "the composing sciences," which, he observes, select only the best materials. Building a house requires good-quality wood, and making clothes requires good-quality wool. Statesmanship must do the same. It must start with good materials if it is to "craft some one power and look" and make a many into a one (308C). The materials here are the two noble but opposed kinds of human beings.

But selecting good human material is far more difficult than choosing good timber or wool. According to the stranger, the statesman-king will test his prospective subjects "in play" in order to see the stuff they're made of (308C-D). He will then hand over the children who pass the test to professionals capable of educating them. The statesman will be the cause that oversees joint-causes, just as weavers supervise carders and all the others who do the prep-work for the weave: he will prescribe, indicate, and command. The purpose of the educators is to form a noble character that the king will appropriate for his act of composing—a character that can participate in courage and moderation.[26] Kingship, we must note, deals harshly with those who ultimately cannot be educated in virtue (the stranger calls them godless and arrogant): it "casts them out by punishing them with death penalties and exiles and the greatest dishonors" (309A). Those who are not violent but "wallow in ignorance"

---

26   Much of the *Republic* is devoted to the education of the guardians and, eventually, to that of the philosopher-kings. In the *Statesman*, by contrast, the stranger never takes up the question of the statesman's education. The statesman is treated simply as the man who already possesses the science of weaving the political web.

kingship puts into the class of slaves. The political art, judging from this passage, is itself an interweaving of the soft and the hard—artful subtlety and unflinching ruthlessness.

Those who are left are the ones whose natures have been "settled in nobility." But nobility, as we have seen, is one-sided or biased. Some noble people are partial to courage, others to moderation. Nobility by itself does not make an individual harmonious and whole: it only makes him courage-shaped or moderation-shaped. Courage and moderation, as separate and opposed noble leanings, are but the material, the beautiful threads, that kingship will interweave to produce the political web. Each offers a necessary power: courage that of solidity or toughness, moderation that of orderliness or grace. The former is the *warp* of the political web, the latter the *woof* (309B).

As the stranger eventually makes clear, the kingly art will weave together the two opposite kinds of noble individuals through forced intermarriage. But the ultimate goal is to interweave the *natures* of courage and moderation in the soul (309B). That is, the statesman-king must produce noble individuals who escape the one-sidedness of their virtue and become genuinely communal or, as we might also say, just.

To answer the earlier question about the manner of kingly interweaving, the stranger distinguishes two kinds of bonds: the divine and the human (309C). The former is the king's act of binding the rational or "eternal-born" part of noble souls with a "genuinely true and steadfast opinion about beautiful and just and good things" and their opposites. The latter binds the "animal-born" part of human nature with "human bonds." These are the marriage arrangements that kingship dictates once the "divine opinion" is in place.

The stranger emphasizes that the statesman and lawgiver "by the muse of kingship" is alone able to produce the bonding of soul to opinion: anyone not able to do this must never be called king or statesman (309C-D). We are not told how this bond is achieved; but once it is there, the courage-loving individual will, because of his true opinion, "grow tame" and become a willing participant in justice, while the one who does not receive this opinion will become a beast (309D-E). Similarly, the order-loving individual, protected by the same true opinion, will become genuinely moderate and intelligent, while the one lacking this opinion will earn a reputation for being simpleminded or naïve.

The stranger repeats his earlier claim that the composing king will not mix bad men with each other or good with bad: such bonding "never proves enduring." The scientific statesman will use as his material only those who proved themselves in the initial test and in the subsequent education in virtue. The stranger here shifts his paradigm, briefly, from weaving to pharmacology. He calls the bond achieved by the true king the *drug* or *potion* that binds together the opposed parts of virtue (310A). It is the antidote that protects noble characters from being too much themselves—even to the point of vice—and the city from falling prey to virtuous excess.

Once the divine bond is in place, the stranger says, the human bonds that govern our animal nature are not difficult either to devise or to enforce. These bonds have to do with intermarriage and procreation. The stranger dismisses marriages that come about for the sake of wealth and power, and focuses on people who marry because they care about family. The problem is that people are by nature attracted to those who are like them and scorn those who are unlike them (310C). They follow "the convenience of the moment." The principle of "like to like" is evident in both how people seek their mates and how they arrange marriages for their children. The stranger is unsparing in his description of the evils that result from this unscientific bonding: marriage of the courageous leads, through continued generations, to madness, and marriage of the moderate to progeny whose souls are torpid and crippled (310D-E). Virtuous characters left to their erotic inclinations, in other words, not only perpetuate their bias through unwise begetting but also cause their virtue to degenerate. Kingly interweaving reverses the erotic direction of becoming (like to like) by enforcing the marriage of opposites.

The stranger approaches his final definition by recalling the human and divine bonds that make the human many into a one. He stresses that the most difficult part of kingly interweaving is the divine bond: the inculcation of "one opinion" about the beautiful and the good in the two noble kinds of soul (310E). This, he says, is the single and whole work of political weaving: to counteract the erotic attraction of like to like through the forced intermarriage of moderate and courageous kinds. The king will bring this about by means of shared opinion, honors and dishonors, reputations, and arranged marriages. The bonding of opposites is the *web* produced by the true statesman and king (311A).

The stranger now returns to the offices that had to be distinguished from kingship. These subordinate levels of rule are to be entrusted to those who share the city's "one opinion" and have overcome the one-sidedness of their virtue. Then the stranger goes higher up the chain of command, to the rulers and supervisors themselves. The statesman here is above and apart from the work of ruling: he selects what sort of rulers the city needs. When it needs one ruler, the political weaver will select someone who has both courage and moderation in his soul, and when it needs more than one, he will mix rulers from each virtuous group. The stranger then reviews, yet again, the evils that result from unmixed virtue. Moderate rulers, he says, are cautious, just, and protective but deficient in vigor and decisiveness. Courageous rulers have the requisite vigor but tend to be unjust and impetuous. Ever wary of how virtuous inclination turns into vice, the stranger concludes that life in a city, whether private or public, will never "turn out beautifully" unless the two opposed characters are present *as a pair* (311B). The need to combine naturally recalcitrant extremes in order to form a mean recalls the earlier discussion of measurement. Indeed, political science, for the stranger, seems in the end to consist largely, if not entirely, in practicing the art of due measure on a grand level.

With this emphasis on the need for due measure in politics, the stranger reaches his final definition. At the end of the *Sophist*, he defined an individual: the trueborn sophist (268C-D). In the *Statesman*, the emphasis is on *statesmanly action* (*praxis*): the statesman as a person does not appear. Rather his "word" has now become "deed": science at work in the thing produced. The end of this action is the weaving together of conflicting virtuous characters. Through its composing science, which imitates the art of weaving, statesmanship produces an invisible web that unites human beings in singlemindedness and friendship. As "the most magnificent and best of all webs" in the realm of communal life, it embraces everyone else in the city, "both slaves and freemen." The political art in this way ensures the city's happiness "to the extent that it befits a city to be happy." Through its rule and supervision, statesmanship leaves nothing out that is essential to this happiness (311C).

Weaving, as we know, is for the sake of the garment produced, a covering that is needed because human beings require protection. The kingly web, in making a human one out of many, does something similar: it wraps human beings in a protective garment in order to make them communal or just (311A). From what does it protect them? One answer is *nature*, which becomes inimical to humankind once god lets go of the cosmic rudder. No longer the beneficiary of yielding nature and divine care, humans become vulnerable and needy. That is why the city contains so many different things—food, containers, furniture, vehicles, tools, and playthings—which minister to human need and desire. Another answer is *virtue*, which, if left natural and naked, that is, unattended by political art, veers off into excess and destroys human life. Human nature also needs protection from *erotic love*, which causes even noble people to chase their like and flee their opposite. Kingly interweaving is exactly what is needed in the Age of Zeus. In this era in which the world goes its own way, human beings, in order to be happy, depend entirely on the godlike figure of the scientific statesman—or rather on the godlike science that weaves the political web.

Young Socrates gets the last word. "Most beautifully," he tells his philosophic mentor, you have completed "the kingly man and statesman." We do not know what he has taken away from this extraordinary talk with the stranger, or whether he has indeed become more dialectical. Nor do we know what the elder Socrates thinks of his kinsman in name, or of the stranger's attempt to define the sophist and the statesman.

Final Reflection

The elder Socrates, we recall, expressed a desire to speak with young Socrates after the boy's conversation with the stranger: he wanted to "get to know his kin" (258A). This reminds us of the beginning of the *Theaetetus*, where Socrates wanted to hear Theodorus tell him about promising students among the youth of Athens (143D). Socrates' interest in Theaetetus and young Socrates takes on a special poignancy when we consider that the dialogues in which these two boys appear are taking place very close to the time of Socrates' trial and death. Shortly before his trial, Socrates, the gadfly of Athens, must surely be wondering into whose hands Athens will fall when he is no longer there. What will be the future of philosophy? What will happen to its nature, spirit, and end in the wake of Socrates? By conversing with his two "kinsmen," Socrates may be searching for a likeness of himself, a likeness that goes beyond physical looks and conventional names. He may want to know whether Athens is capable of producing another individual who will be passionate about inquiry and who will care for the city's virtue.

The strangely anonymous stranger, whom Socrates compared to a god of refutation (*Sophist* 216B), arrives in Athens with an air that combines courtesy and confidence. He is deferential toward Socrates, but he also seems sure that he can go beyond Socratic perplexity, knowledge of ignorance, and erotic striving for wisdom. The stranger may be the philosophic wave of the future, the embodiment of a new version of philosophy that is more positive, more rigorously technical, more scientific, than the erotic (and politically dangerous) version that Socrates lived. It is possible that Theaetetus and young Socrates, who work very well with the stranger, are more suited to his philosophic "way" than to that of Socrates.

Whether or not these reflections point in the right direction, it seems clear that the *Sophist* and *Statesman* set up an implicit opposition between Socrates and the stranger. They invite us to examine how the stranger might indeed go beyond Socrates in some respects, while falling short of him in others. The comparison of Socrates and the stranger takes us back to the question with which the projected trilogy began, and which Plato wants us to keep asking: Who is the philosopher?

APPENDIX A: THE ART OF WEAVING

Weaving is devoted above all to producing protective wrap-arounds, cloaks bound together by the same material of which they are made—in this dialogue, wool. The preparation consists of a) carding or combing, separating the wool to straighten the fibers and remove impurities, and b) spinning, twisting together the fibers of the carded wool held on a forked stick, the distaff, from which the wool is drawn into thread wound onto a spindle. At the end of the spindle there is a spindle whorl that acts as a fly-wheel to give torque to the woman's twisting of the fibers in her fingers.

Two types of thread are needed: a solid tightly-spun *warp*, hung vertically from the upright loom frame and held taut by conical loom weights, and the softer looser *woof*, to be passed horizontally through the warp threads.

The weaving itself consists of a) the woman's walking back and forth before the loom as she interweaves the warp and the woof, and b) pushing the warp thread upward with a rod to tighten the weaving. The cloth making is completed by fulling—washing and brushing the web to give it density and nap.

Thus, weaving as a whole involves separating, combining, and intertwining.

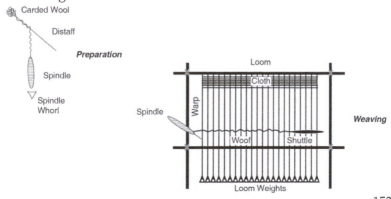

153

Appendix B: The Divisions of Plato's *Statesman*

The divisions of the *Statesman* pretty well trace out the expositional structure of the whole dialogue. The longest is the first. Its terms set the course of the search for the true statesman.

Yet it is the pursuit of divisions itself that turns out to be the real object of the effort. For, as the stranger announces almost precisely at the center of the discussion (285D), the *diairesis* is being carried out for the sake of becoming "more dialectical." Dialectic, however, is discerning thinking, and its means—supplemented by myth (268D) and paradigm (277D)—is *division-and-collection*. Serendipitously, this very means reveals the statesman's art to be just like itself, for the statesman manages his charges' opposing temperaments by *separating and interweaving* (305E). Thus, an exercise in dialectic turns out to be, after all, a preparation for ruling.

Initial Attempt: A Partly Misleading Path to the Statesman (258C-266D, recap. 267A)

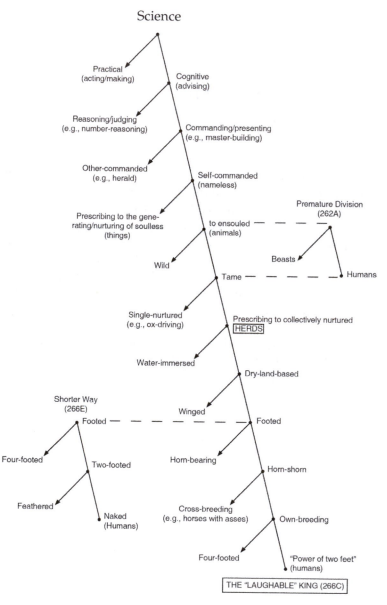

Science

Practical
(acting/making)

Cognitive
(advising)

Reasoning/judging
(e.g., number-reasoning)

Commanding/presenting
(e.g., master-building)

Other-commanded
(e.g., herald)

Self-commanded
(nameless)

Premature Division
(262A)

Prescribing to the gene-
rating/nurturing of soulless
(things)

to ensouled — — —
(animals)

Beasts

Wild

Tame — — — — Humans

Single-nurtured
(e.g., ox-driving)

Prescribing to collectively nurtured
HERDS

Water-immersed

Dry-land-based

Shorter Way
(266E)
Footed — — — — — — Footed

Winged

Four-footed

Two-footed

Horn-bearing

Horn-shorn

Feathered

Naked
(Humans)

Cross-breeding
(e.g., horses with asses)

Own-breeding

Four-footed

"Power of two feet"
(humans)

THE "LAUGHABLE" KING (266C)

FIGURE 1

A Partial Revision (275C-276E)

After this initial attempt, we get the myth of the self-reversing world, which delineates the difference between the divine and the human king. The stranger now returns to the work of division. He picks up at "nurtured" in Figure 1, now named "tending" or "caregiving."

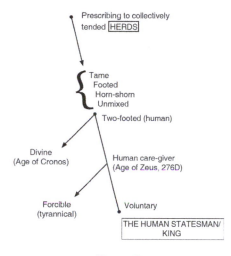

Prescribing to collectively tended HERDS

{ Tame
  Footed
  Horn-shorn
  Unmixed

Two-footed (human)

Divine
(Age of Cronos)

Human care-giver
(Age of Zeus, 276D)

Forcible
(tyrannical)

Voluntary

THE HUMAN STATESMAN/
KING

FIGURE 2

The stranger then presents the paradigm of weaving, which is intended both to distinguish the care-giving king from his false contenders and to serve as a model for the art of statesmanship (279A).

Weaving: A Paradigm for Statesmanship (279B-285C)
CLOAKS I

Things Crafted

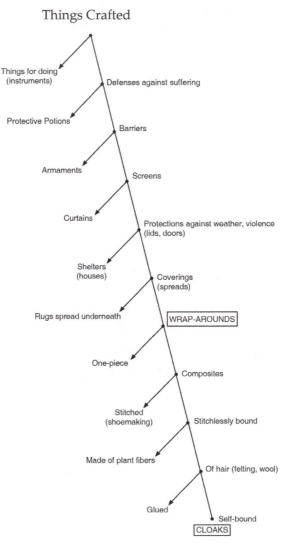

FIGURE 3A

Notes:

1. For the arts, the first division was: Practical/Cognitive. For their products it is: Instrumental/Defensive.
2. As cloak-working is (mostly) identical with weaving, so kingship is identical with statesmanship (280A).

3. The division of Figure 3a is followed by a recapitulation intended to "remove" (280D) the irrelevant sheltering arts. It is reported from the bottom up, except that WRAP-AROUNDS are listed first, presumably because this heading introduces the sought-for paradigm character of cloaks: they envelop the human body as the statesman's art wraps in its web the political body (311C).

CLOAKS II

List of Arts Contending With Weaving for Taking Care of Woolen Cloaks:
Carding (Combing)
Warp-and-woof making (spinning)
Brushing, washing, mending, (fulling, 282A)
and
Instrument-making: "joint-causes" (281C)

Woolen Cloaks (Cause)

Joint causes
(list of contending arts)

Proper cause
(weaving itself)

FIGURE 3B

The joint-causes appear throughout the divisions of

The Art of Weaving Woolen Cloaks

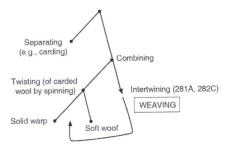

Separating
(e.g., carding)

Combining

Twisting (of carded
wool by spinning)

Intertwining (281A, 282C)

WEAVING

Solid warp

Soft woof

FIGURE 3C

Note: Weaving, the Art of Cloak-making, is thus the re-combination of final divisions, the twisting together of solid warp and soft woof.

But why take the long route of Cloaks I, when we could have gone the shorter way of Cloaks II? This question leads to the art of due measure (285A) and a division of all arts under

The Art of Measurement

Magnitudes measured in relation to their opposites (e.g., long vs. short accounts)

Measured in relation to due measure, the fitting (e.g., the needful length)

Figure 4

The Genuine Statesman and His Imitators (285C-303C)

Back to the king and his contenders (287B), now qualified by the stranger's announcement that these divisions are being made less for the sake of finding the king than for young Socrates' becoming more dialectical. To separate the true king from his contenders the stranger divides the arts in the city into joint-causes and the true political cause—statesmanship. The mode of dividing is not necessarily dual, any more than it was for the paradigmatic joint-causes of weaving.

The division picks up from "nurturing" or "care-giving" at the beginning of Figure 2.

Arts in the City

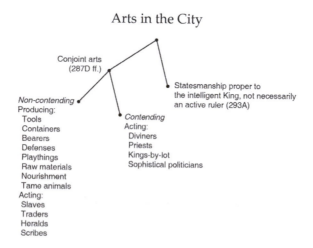

Conjoint arts (287D ff.)

Non-contending
Producing:
Tools
Containers
Bearers
Defenses
Playthings
Raw materials
Nourishment
Tame animals
Acting:
Slaves
Traders
Heralds
Scribes

Contending
Acting:
Diviners
Priests
Kings-by-lot
Sophistical politicians

Statesmanship proper to the intelligent King, not necessarily an active ruler (293A)

Figure 5

The true king's contender is pursued in three stages:

Stage One: A false start—an attempt to elucidate the division that will mark off the false contender by distinguishing

Five Types of Political Rule (291D ff.)

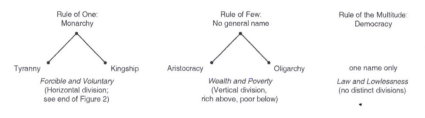

FIGURE 6

Conclusion (292D): This set of distinctions (Forcible/Voluntary, Wealth/Poverty, Law/Lawlessness) is not the proper criterion for separating the true king from his pretenders. That criterion must be the presence of *science* in ruling human beings (292D). Since it has been affirmed that kingship is a supervisory science (260A, 292B), it is possible to lay out a different division by Art and Artlessness of rule, that is, rule *with science* and rule *without science*.

Stage Two: The correct division into

Six Types of Political Rule (301A)

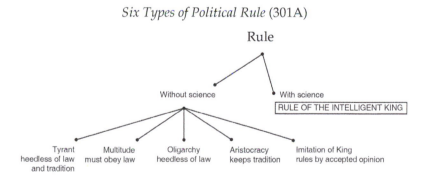

FIGURE 7

Note: Although the stranger at this point has six regimes, he prefers to name them as only five, giving the name "kingship" to both true kingship and its imitation (301A-B).

The next question is: Which of the artless regimes is the least, and which the most, burdensome? The stranger returns to the three regimes of Figure 6, divides Democracy, and adds the true King, to get seven types in all.

Stage Three: Worst, and best, regime chosen from

Seven Types of Political Rule (302B)

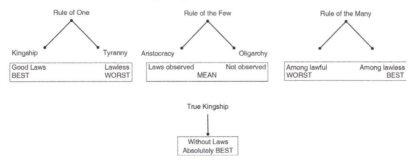

Figure 8

The most serious pretender (see Figure 5) has now been located as a usurper of the true king in six of the seven defined regimes, for all rulers except the true king are "not statesmen" but "the greatest of sophists" (303C).

The Well-Ordered City (303C-311C)

Now the more honorable pretenders—the functionaries within the regime—must be partitioned off and assigned their proper places. To accomplish this, the stranger declares a *hierarchy of sciences*. The science that determines whether other sciences are to be learned and applied must rule the sciences that teach and act (304C).

Honorable Arts in the City (304D)

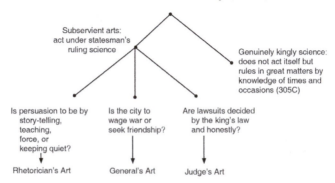

Figure 9

What, finally, is the king's actual knowledge? The stranger's answer to this question begins with an "astonishing" claim that parts of virtue oppose each other.

Virtue (306B)

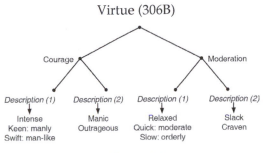

FIGURE 10

Note: The figure shows two kinds of opposition: Virtue is divided into the opposing virtues of courage and moderation, each of which is opposed to itself with respect to praise and blame.

The statesman has to compose temperaments that by themselves risk slavery and destruction from slackness and aggression. The stranger therefore returns to his paradigm to distinguish the functions of political weaving.

The King as Weaver (307E)

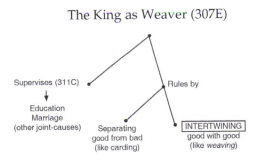

FIGURE 11

Note: At the end of the dialogue, the stranger represents the true king as a weaver who not only intertwines different temperaments but also weaves all the citizens into a web, which, like the self-bound Wrap-around Cloak of Figure 3a, envelops the whole city in unanimity and friendship (309C).

BIBLIOGRAPHY

Texts and Translations Most Frequently Consulted

Benardete, S. 1986. *Plato's* Statesman, Part III of *The Being of the Beautiful*. Translated and with Commentary. Chicago: University of Chicago Press.

Brann, E., Kalkavage, P., Salem, E. 1996. *Plato's* Sophist, *Or the Professor of Wisdom*. Translation, with Introduction and Glossary. Newburyport, MA: Focus Publishing.

Burnet, J. 1900. *Politicus* in Platonis Opera: Vol. I. Oxford: Clarendon Press.

Campbell, L. 1867. *The* Sophistes *and* Politicus *of Plato, With a Revised Text and English Notes*. Oxford: Clarendon Press.

Fowler, H. N. 1962. *Plato*: Statesman *and* Philebus. Cambridge, MA: Loeb Classical Library, Harvard University Press. (Facing Greek and English)

Rowe, C. J. 1999. *Plato*: Statesman. Translated with Introduction. Indianapolis: Hackett Publishing.

Skemp, J. B. 1961. *Plato's* Statesman: *A Translation of the* Politicus *of Plato with Introductory Essays and Footnotes*. New Haven: Yale University Press.

Waterfield, Robin. 1995. Plato: *Statesman*. Edited by Julia Annas and Robin Waterfield. Cambridge: Cambridge University Press.

Selected Works on the *Statesman*

Brumbaugh, R. S. "Diction and Dialectic: The Language and Thought of Plato's Stranger from Elea," in Robb, K. 1983. *Language and Thought in Early Greek Philosophy*.

Klein, J. 1977. *Plato's Trilogy*: Theaetetus, *the* Sophist, *and the* Statesman. Chicago: University of Chicago Press.

Miller, M. 2004. *The Philosopher in Plato's* Statesman. Together with

"Dialectical Education and Unwritten Teachings in Plato's *Statesman.*" Parmenides Publishing.

Rosen, S. 1995. *Plato's* Statesman: *The Web of Politics,* New Haven: Yale University Press.

Zuckert, C. H. 2009. *Plato's Philosophers: The Coherence of the Dialogues.* Chicago: University of Chicago Press.